Visual Tools

for constructing knowledge

David Hyerle

Association for Supervision and Curriculum Development
Alexandria, Virginia

Association for Supervision and Curriculum Development
1250 N. Pitt Street • Alexandria, Virginia 22314-1453
Telephone: (703) 549-9110 • Fax: (703) 299-8631

Gene R. Carter, *Executive Director*
Michelle Terry, *Assistant Executive Director, Program
  Development*
Ronald S. Brandt, *Assistant Executive Director*
Nancy Modrak, *Managing Editor, ASCD Books*
Carolyn R. Pool, *Associate Editor*
René Bahrenfuss, *Copy Editor*
Carly Rothman, *Project Assistant*
Gary Bloom, *Manager, Design and Production Services*
Karen Monaco, *Senior Designer*
Tracey A. Smith, *Print Production Coordinator*
Cynthia Stock, *Desktop Publisher*

ASCD publications present a variety of viewpoints. The
views expressed or implied in this book should not be interpreted as official positions of the Association.

Printed in the United States of America.
ASCD Stock No. 196072
pc7/96
Price: $18.95

Library of Congress Cataloging-in-Publication Data
Hyerle, David
    Visual tools for constructing knowledge / David Hyerle.
        p. cm.
    Includes bibliographical references and index.
    ISBN 0-87120-266-2 (alk. paper)
    1. Visual learning. 2. Constructivism (Education) 3. Thought and
thinking. 4. Critical thinking. 5. Cognition. I. Title.
    LB1067.5.H94   1996
    370.15′2—dc20   96-20381
                                                            CIP

00 99 98 97 96   5 4 3 2 1

Visual Tools for Constructing Knowledge

Foreword v
   Frances Faircloth Jones

Prologue vii
   Arthur L. Costa

Introduction: The Forest and the Trees 1

1 Why Visual Tools Now? 7

2 Introducing Visual Tools 21

3 Brainstorming Webs 35

4 Task-Specific Organizers 51

5 Thinking-Process Maps 71

6 Thinking Maps: A Common Visual Language
   for Learning 95

7 Visual Tools for Lifelong Learning 117

References 128

Selected Resources for Visual Tools 132

Index 134

About the Author

David Hyerle is Director of Curriculum and Professional Development with the Innovative Learning Group, a Division of Innovative Sciences, Inc., Cary, North Carolina. He is also chairperson for the Board of Directors of Educators for Social Responsibility.

Hyerle continues to deepen the Thinking Maps® approach described in this book and to investigate the use of other visual tools through practice and research in classrooms. He is interested in collecting examples of student and teacher applications of different types of visual tools. Please send exemplars and queries to:

David Hyerle
Innovative Sciences, Inc.
P.O. Box 5509
Cary, NC 27511
Phone: 1-800-243-9169
e-mail: ILG@valley.net
WWW: http://www.thinkingmaps.com

Foreword

Can you draw thinking? Can you sing it? Can you sculpt it? Are these crazy questions?

Not according to David Hyerle and Art Costa and a distinguished procession of ASCD writers and thinkers. From a program called TACTICS for Thinking, to a book called *Dimensions of Thinking* and another titled *Developing Minds*, to the books and professional development programs of the Dimensions of Learning program, ASCD has led thousands of teachers and students in many countries to develop—and draw—the dimensions and shapes and directions of their thinking. Not only can you draw thinking, but music helps you think, according to other ASCD authors who have described how the brain works.

As Hyerle points out, the brain works by making patterns; and we can visualize this process through a medium called "visual tools." Many of us have used the three types of visual tools that Hyerle discusses: *brainstorming webs, task-specific organizers, and thinking-process maps*. If you flip through this book, you will see many diagrams you will instantly recognize; but please read the text to see *why* you and your students should use them, and *how* to get the most out of these tools.

The author provides sample lessons, assessments, and "portraits" of visual tools in action. He emphasizes the interdisciplinary nature of making patterns, as well as the collaborative construction of knowledge—as teachers and students create their own tools and use computer software programs as guides and coaches in ways to manage the information overflow we all experience. He discusses the use of visual tools within the framework of three themes:

- *constructivism* as a paradigm for learning;
- the *types, uses, and successes* of visual tools; and
- a vision of *integrating* teaching, learning, and assessing using visual tools.

Through "concept mapping," "fishbone diagrams," "Thinking Maps," and the "feedback loops" of systems thinking, Hyerle shows us how schools are becoming true learning organizations—and fostering lifelong learning among students and teachers. One caution he expresses is also an exciting prospect: "We are still in the discovery phase of learning about how knowledge is actually constructed."

There is a map of this book in the introduction, and even a map of the prologue, by Art Costa. Check them out. You may want to draw a map of your own reflections and understandings!

FRANCES FAIRCLOTH JONES
ASCD President, 1996–97

Prologue

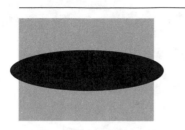

Deeply rooted in constructivist theory, this book draws on philosophical and psychological models of how the mind works, how human intellectual capacities emerge and grow over time, how humans derive meaning, and how knowledge is structured. The intent is to provide educators with insights into how interventions can be arranged and conditions organized so as to educe, enhance, and refine those human intellectual resources.

In reviewing this book and preparing to write this prologue, I reminisced about other constructivist theorists who influenced the formation of my views of learning and human cognitive development: Bruner, Piaget, Taba, Suchman, Feuerstein. I retrieved several of the constructivist mental models that scaffolded their philosophical and psychological search. I found myself returning to Jerome Bruner's compelling inquiry, "What makes human beings human?" I began to mentally reflect on and list some of those unique intellectual capacities that distinguish humans from other life forms.

When I approached the upper limits of my memory span—that magical number 7 (plus or minus 2) items to hold in my head simultaneously—I realized I had to write them down or

What Makes Humans Human?

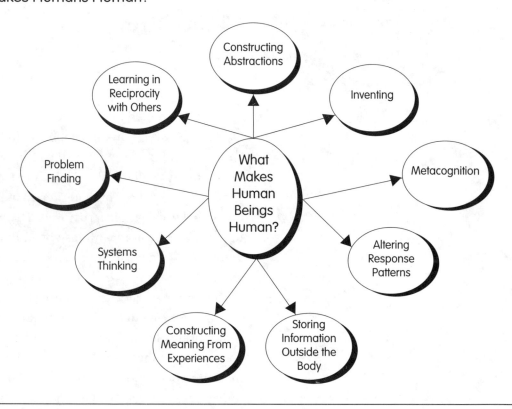

some might drop out. I therefore represented my thoughts graphically (Figure 1).

As I mapped, I also came to realize that what I thought in my head was fuzzier than what I wrote on paper. As I refined what was on paper, I mutually refined my inner thoughts. I realized, for example, that many human capacities, while innate within us, are underdeveloped and will need to be amplified to live productively in the future. Not only did the brainstorming map allow me to see the relationships between these attributes, but it also disclosed overlaps, redundancies, and omissions. I edited here and there to become consistent and then reflected on my map. I felt satisfied that I had a structure that could be decorated with a few insightful contributions about the benefits and potentials of this book. Using the structure, I then turned to composing. As the thoughts flowed from my brain and were translated to individual letters by my fingers and flowed as words onto the computer screen, I again revisited my

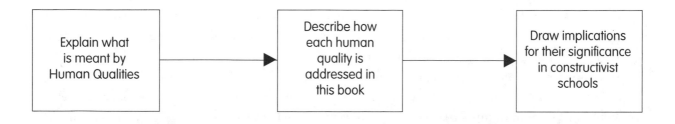

Figure 2

Prologue Process

map—altering here and there, combining where necessary, and generating more bubbles as additional thoughts emerged that, in turn, stimulated others.

The gift that David Hyerle has bestowed on us in this book, you see, is a set of tools for exploring, enhancing, and refining those unique cognitive qualities of humanness. I would like to:

- Explain what is meant by each of these uniquely human qualities that undergird constructivist theory.
- Describe how Hyerle has so masterfully addressed them.
- Make implications for their significance to constructivist schools where the staff is intent on emancipating themselves, their students, and their communities from the shackles of nearly a century of reductionism (see Figure 2).

The following nine human qualities, then, may illuminate my reflections on this book.

1. **Metacognition:** To the best of our knowledge, human beings are the only form of life that can reflect on their own thinking processes. Basically, metacognition means that, when confronted with a dilemma or some obstacle, humans draw on their mental resources to plan a course of action, monitor that strategy while executing it, then reflect on the strategy to evaluate its productiveness in terms of the outcomes it was intended to achieve.

The "thinking" visual tools described in this book are forms of metacognition—graphically displayed thinking processes.

We know that what distinguishes expert from novice problem solvers is habituated metacognition; that thinking and discussing thinking begets more thinking; and that thinking and problem-solving capacities are enhanced when students think aloud, discuss, and communicate their thought processes to others—when students make their implicit problem-solving processes explicit.

2. **Constructing Abstractions:** Humans have the unique capacity to synopsize massive amounts of information and to shape raw data into workable patterns. There was a time when human beings lacked access to information in making decisions. Data were scarce, took long periods of time to transmit, and were simplistic in format and immediate in implication. With the advent of the Information Age, however, an overwhelming amount of immediately accessible and often conflicting information became available. Because of the lack of vast amounts of disparate, available information in the past, the human intellectual capacity for constructing abstractions may have been underdeveloped. And because of the increase in available information, the upper limits of this capacity will be continually tested and exceeded in the future.

This book provides visual tools to assist learners to organize and find patterns among the overwhelming amount of information available today, as well as to make sense out of it and evaluate it.

To live productively in the future, we have found that the capacity to construct abstractions has become prerequisite to survival and will need to be grown. Resourceful humans, therefore, will continue to develop their capacity to gather, organize, make sense out of, and evaluate the overabundance of technology-generated and -transmitted data.

3. **Storing Information Outside the Body:** I recently had more memory installed in my computer. It was a simple process of installing more DIMMs (dual inline memory modules). I wish I could do the same for my brain!

Human beings are the only form of life that can store, organize, and retrieve data in locations other than our bodies. This human capacity probably emerged as a survival mechanism because our ancestors reached the limits of their memory span. They had the need to remember and communicate an increasing amount of information and therefore used tools to record and convey mental visions and concepts. Cave walls, where their dwellers formed their marks and petroglyphs, may be history's first storage locations. Now videotapes, museums, libraries, microfiche, computers, and CD-ROMs assist in accomplishing this human function.

This book fulfills this human intellectual capacity by providing tools to generate, store, and communicate information in such a manner that can be recalled and interpreted at a later time and by others.

Because the archives of the mind are limited and the amount of information is increasing, students will need to learn strategies of harvesting, storing, cataloging, retrieving, interpreting, and communicating vast amounts of information among locations beyond their brains.

4. **Systems Thinking:** Humans have the unique capacity to see the parts in relation to the whole and thus to see patterns, congruences, and inconsistencies. Human preferences for perceiving parts *or* wholes as separate cognitive inclinations, as some cognitive-style theorists would have us believe, is inadequate for productive participation in a quantum world. In dynamic systems, tiny inputs can reverberate throughout the system, producing dramatically large consequences. Systems thinking fulfills a

human capacity to understand the boundaries within a part of the total system and, at the same time, to understand the interactions with its interconnecting parts.

Hyerle suggests the use of visual tools to guide thinking when we need to simultaneously pay attention to the whole and analyze whether the parts are, indeed, interdependent and interconnected. Visual tools are one way to describe how a system functions when altered or when innovative thinking in one part of the system has an effect on the total system. Maps serve as tools for examining many processes and interactions, such as how decisions are made, how disciplines work together, how new practices are initiated, and how priorities are established.

Families, weather systems, and national economies are examples of systems. To participate fully in any society and to protect a fragile environment, citizens must realize that any system is a synergistic relationship of interlocking parts; as one part changes, it has an effect on the other parts. No one part can operate efficiently unless the other parts of the system work in harmony. This capacity for simultaneously holonomous parts-whole relationships has become essential, not only in the workplace, but also in solving environmental and social problems.

5. Problem Finding: To the best of our knowledge, humans are the only form of life that actually enjoys the search for problems to solve. Being dissatisfied with existing levels of certainty, humans have an insatiable passion for doubting the status quo, sensing ambiguities, and detecting anomalies. Once having intu-

ited such inconsistencies, humans have developed the profound capacity to engage in experimental inquiry, to set up procedures to test and evaluate alternative ideas, and to strive for certitude. The process of modern scientific thought thrives on this human tendency.

Maps are tools for displaying intellectual processes: the clustering of the diverse, complex procedures of experimentation. They represent the sequences, alternative branches, choice points, and pathways that surround the acquisition and production of knowledge. These become the basis for systematic inquiry and scientific investigation.

Process is, in fact, the highest form of learning and the most appropriate base for curriculum change. In the teaching of process, we can best portray learning as a perpetual endeavor and not something that terminates with the end of school. Through process, we can employ knowledge, not merely as a composite of information, but as a system for continuous learning (Parker and Rubin 1966).

6. Reciprocal Learning: Human beings are social beings having a compulsive craving to engage with others. The most hideous form of punishment is to deprive humans of their quest for reciprocity. Humans learn best in groups. Intelligence gets shaped through interaction with others—justifying reasons, resolving differences, actively listening to another person's point of view, achieving consensus, and receiving feedback.

In this book, Hyerle commends interactivity as tools are developed in cooperative settings. Such tools assist in developing students' and teachers' capacity for flexibility—viewing situations from multiple perspectives, as well as being able to change and adapt based on feedback from others. Using such cooperative tools transcends the sense of self—enlarging the conception of "me" to a sense of "us." And becoming less attached to egocentric orientations permits us to exercise more advanced reasoning processes. Use of such tools provides interconnectedness and kinship that comes from a unity of being, a sense of sharing, and a mutual bonding to common goals and shared values. Students understand that as we transcend the self and become part of the whole, we do not lose our individuality; rather, we relinquish our egocentricity.

Collaboration, cooperation, and interdependence are paramount not only in today's work cultures but also in families, in governmental organizations, and among nations. Schools must enhance students' capacities for holding their own values and actions in abeyance and to lend their energies and resources to the achievement of group goals; to contribute themselves to a common good; and to seek collegiality and draw on the resources of others. Students must come to regard conflict as valuable, trusting their abilities to manage group differences in productive ways, to seek feedback from others as a valued source of learning. They must know that "all of us" is more efficient than any "one of us." Interdependence makes possible the most complete and effective intellectual functioning of human beings.

7. **Inventing:** Human beings are creative—they are toolmakers. Although some other life forms may perceive the need for and employ instruments to accomplish tasks and solve problems, humans are the only form of life capable of designing and creating new tools.

Further, humans are intrinsically rather than extrinsically motivated, working on the task because of the aesthetic challenge, rather than the material rewards. They constantly strive for greater fluency, elaboration, novelty, parsimony, simplicity, craftsmanship, perfection, beauty, harmony, and balance.

Hyerle disparages giving students ready-made maps to follow and fill in. He emphasizes the need for students to invent their own tools and to hone and refine them as they generate and gather information, process or elaborate that information into conceptual relationships, and then apply and evaluate those generalizations. He believes strongly that there is an inherent motivation within each of us for this inventive process, which can be capacitated through such visual toolmaking.

All humans have the capacity to generate novel, original, clever, or ingenious products, solutions, and techniques. We often try to conceive problem solutions differently, examining alternative possibilities from many angles. We tend to project ourselves into different roles using metaphors and analogies, starting with a vision and working backward, imagining we are the objects being considered. Creative people take risks—they "live on the edge of their competence," testing their limits—if that capacity is developed.

8. Deriving Meaning from Experiences: Thomas A. Edison stated that he never made a mistake; he only learned from experience. One of the most significant attributes that makes humans human is their capacity for reflecting on and learning from their experiences. Intelligent people form feelings and impressions about an event; they compare intentions with accomplishments; they analyze why events turned out as they did; they search for causal factors that produced the effects; they summarize their impressions; and, based on those analyses, they project how they could modify their actions in the future.

The human mind, however, is inclined to distort or delete information to suit its own purposes and biases. Hyerle suggests that the use of maps as tools for reflection can assist us by graphically tracking the procedures employed in an event. Reflecting on the visual pathways, strategies, and decisions is a more efficient and systematic way of holding information than attempting to recall it. The experience can be analyzed more honestly and completely if it has been graphically organized.

Autonomous individuals set personal goals and are self-directing, self-monitoring, and self-modifying. Because they are constantly experimenting and experiencing, they fail frequently—but they *fail forward*, learning from the situation. A major outcome for any school desirous of preparing autonomous humans, is to develop students' capacities for continuous self-analysis, self-improvement, self-referencing, self-evaluation, and self-modification.

9. Altering Response Patterns: Whereas other forms of life are "wired" to respond in certain ways to stimuli in their environment, humans are self-actualizing and self-modifying—they can consciously and deliberately make choices about whether and how they wish to respond. They can alter their habits and can voluntarily select among alternative responses. Whereas we might be inclined to be impulsive, we can choose to be deliberative; if we are disposed to make premature evaluations, we can choose to withhold our judgments; when we are habituated into perceiving egocentrically, we can choose to perceive allocentrically. This decision-making process requires consciousness and flexibility—being aware of our own and other's actions and drawing on a repertoire of response patterns.

Hyerle supports the use of visual tools because they encourage consciousness and flexibility of responses. Deliberately employing mapping tools causes us to restrain our impulsivity, to suspend our judgments, to generate and consider alternatives, and to attend empathically to others' perspectives.

Fully functioning humans engage in continuous learning. If our students believe that their education has been completed on graduation, they've missed the whole point of schooling. Continuous lifespan learning is essential for students today and in the future. With advances in technology and changes in the workplace and human mobility, we may find other underdeveloped capacities—continuing to learn how to learn, how to change and grow, and how to relinquish old patterns and acquire new ones.

***

David Hyerle also proposes that the use of these tools is not just "kid stuff." Cooperatively inventing and employing such tools benefits the human intellectual capacities of the adults in the school as well. When the staff design, generate, and employ these maps, they too become more aware of their data-generating, storing, and retrieval systems. All staff members are at once beneficiaries and leaders of the learning organization. They more readily see the parts-whole relationship. They view their particular operation as part of a larger whole and see that innovative/creative thinking in one part of the system has an effect on the total system. Everybody in the entire system is perceived to be a continual learner—a caring, thinking individual capable of complex decision making, creativity,

problem solving, and continued intellectual development.

The use of visual tools throughout the school will have a corresponding and salutary effect on the development of the adult intelligences and capacities that may be prerequisite to the development of student's capacities. Indeed, we are all learners in a learning organization. What gives integrity and coherence to school life is not only the continuity and use of visual tools across departments and grade levels, but also the use of a shared, common language throughout the organization. Perhaps it is this fractal quality that is the unique characteristic of an intelligent school.

Reference

Parker, J.C., and L.J. Rubin. (1966). *Process as Content: Curriculum Design and the Application of Knowledge.* Chicago: Rand McNally.

ARTHUR L. COSTA
Professor Emeritus, California State University
Co-director, Institute for Intelligent Behavior
Berkeley, California

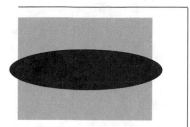

Introduction: The Forest and the Trees

The dynamic use of visual tools to construct and explicitly show knowledge first surfaced in schools in the late '70s and early '80s, mostly through the use of brainstorming "webs." This was when I began visually linking ideas, first as a student, then as a teacher.

During my senior year at the University of California at Berkeley, I became interested in the teaching of writing and took a course with the Bay Area Writing Project that included learning how to use webbing techniques. After creating a few tentative doodles and an ungraceful spaghetti of zig-zag lines, I began to develop my own personal language and use the webbing techniques for my other courses. Classmates peeked at my notes quizzically. My control over ideas and writing quickly improved. My first major success came when I "mapped out" a binder full of lecture and research notes for an upcoming final exam onto one horizontal summary page.

As I worked through the exam—which was composed of page after page of unrelenting multiple-choice and short- and long-answer questions—I was able to "pull up" this blueprint in my mind and access connected theories and details and, ultimately, mostly correct responses. This experience showed me that I could construct my own view of information. I could see, simultaneously, the forest *and* the trees, the macro-vision of the whole subject as expressed in the complex micro-vision of interrelated details.

Some years later I began teaching at an inner-city middle school in Oakland, California, and slowly introduced webbing to my students. They soon were comfortable with visual brainstorming techniques and had breakthrough successes with the quantity of ideas they could web. There was also a richer texture and personal detail to their ideas and a better final product, especially when balanced with instruction and practice in holistic scoring, group editing, and traditional writing techniques.

I was soon enthralled by these simple tools because webbing opened new windows into the mindscapes of my students' idiosyncratic thinking patterns. Students could externalize and safely show their interrelated thinking patterns; I could see what was once internal, invisible, inaccessible. I finally could view what *and* how each student was thinking about the content I taught—and I also discovered certain problems.

Students' maps often revealed a storm of clouded concepts. But these clouds were a point of learning, an opportunity. I could access and assess my students' misconceptions and their confusion about how to further organize, prioritize, delete, and clarify the overwhelming amount of associated ideas they had drawn. Students could always brainstorm bursts of exciting and imaginative ideas, but their organiza-

tion for a completed piece of writing did not always match the power of their ideas and my expectations for a well-crafted paper. Though I kept going back to traditional outlining because it was a steady, known anchor, I began questioning, "What happens after the storm?"

About this time I began piloting a "thinking skills" program that included diagrams based on several thinking processes. I also read about different techniques based on students using more structured mapping for concept development. These experiences—and the school's tentative moves toward a "thinking curriculum"—brought me to a tantalizing question. What would happen if teachers and students had basic maps for applying different, fundamental thinking processes? I began practicing with the idea of specifically linking mapping with basic patterns of thinking. Could we support students and teachers in explicitly transferring thinking processes across content areas?

Communication and even in-the-moment assessment in the classroom might change. Student-centered learning might be enhanced if students had their own visual tools. Teachers might gain valuable insights into their students' ideas and misconceptions. Teachers might ask higher-order questions with a realistic expectation that students had tools for responding.

And I also wondered: If teachers simply asked more higher-order questions, would students have the tools to respond to them? It was clear from my students' brainstorming webs that they could generate linked ideas. But could they analyze, synthesize, and evaluate their own thinking? By the late 1980s, I was writing curriculum materials for teachers, and in the process I developed a common visual language of eight flexible tools called Thinking Maps®. This language of visual tools evolved from experiences with other teachers and has been enriched through research and practice over the years.

Working with teachers across the country over the past decade, I have become intrigued by another type of visual tool called "graphic organizers." These organizers vary from text-structure diagrams for comparing characters in a reading comprehension assignment, to "fish-bone" cause-and-effect formats in the social sciences, to traditional Venn diagrams for classifying in science, to detailed flowcharts for mathematics and computer instruction. There is a seemingly endless variety.

Over the past 15 years, through the investigation of all these different kinds of visual tools, I have enjoyed collecting ideas and techniques from teachers, curriculum developers, and researchers. It is a rare teacher, having used a visual tool, who does not rave about its success. I believe this enthusiasm also reflects a rewarding outcome of using these tools in classrooms: Students enjoy the process of opening their minds and showing not only *what* they are thinking (content) but also *how* they are working through complex questions (process).

At this time, visual tools are showing up in schools in texts, books of blackline masters for organizers, professional development programs, software, and tests. I have witnessed excitement about visual tools, as well as confusion. These tools come in many different forms. Teachers usually use one type of tool because it has

worked with students, which means they and their students are missing opportunities to gain control of the wide range of visual tools. Many of these lost opportunities can be recovered in this book as we investigate the question: What are the different types of visual tools, and how are they used in classrooms and across whole schools?

My "big picture" response to this question is the organization of visual tools into three basic categories: brainstorming webs, task-specific organizers, and thinking-process maps. The definition of visual tools, examples of these three types of tools, and ideas for how to use them are the core of this book. As you read and scan the figures, you may not agree with my categories as shown, because categories are usually subjective classifications. But I have attempted to bring exemplars of these successful tools into one volume. I hope this work will help clarify the field and inspire others to pursue further investigations.

In addition, several "big picture," theoretical themes are woven through this book, based on other questions: What are the long-term, developmental implications for constructing and assessing knowledge when students have these visual tools? How is the *form* of knowledge structured in different ways using the designs offered by different visual tools? And do visual tools offer new forms, or languages, for meeting the needs of learners working in an Information Age where constructivism is the guiding educational paradigm and the Information Superhighway is the new metaphor for information access? Simply, could these tools provide a

FIGURE I.1

Tree Map

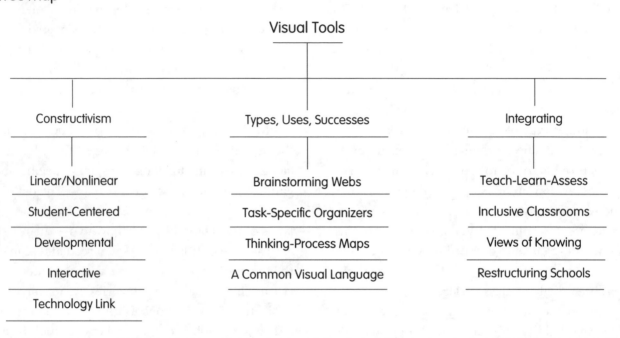

much needed foundation for restructuring, from the ground up, how teachers and students communicate in schools?

Ultimately, I hope this book opens a dialogue about all these questions to support students, teachers, and administrators in this transitional period. It is time that we—learners all—see both the forest and the trees.

Maps of This Book

In the spirit of this investigation of visual tools, some of the key points in this book are represented using visual tools. For example, the book's organization is presented in two figures through two Thinking Maps®, not in traditional outline form. The first map, a Tree Map, shows the overall conceptual picture of the book in hierarchical structure (Figure I.1). Three major themes drive the text:

- *constructivism* as a paradigm for learning;
- the *types, uses, and successes* of visual tools; and
- a vision of *integrating* teaching, learning, and assessing using visual tools (Novak and Gowin 1984).

These points lead to the long-term purposes of displaying alternative views of knowing and thus restructuring, from the ground up, how

FIGURE I.2

Flow Map

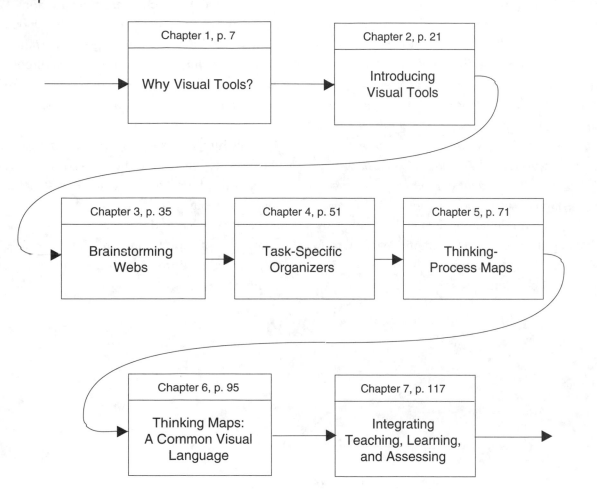

participants in a learning community develop ideas, communicate, and negotiate meanings.

These three major areas of interest return throughout the text and roughly correspond to the flow of the chapters, shown in the Flow Map (Figure I.2). Chapters 1 and 2 are investigations of why visual tools are now being used, fol-lowed by the definition of visual tools and the three types. Key concerns, questions, and sug-gestions for bringing visual tools into class-rooms conclude Chapter 2, which leads to deeper consideration of each type of visual tool.

Chapters 3 through 5 specifically detail the three types of visual tools: brainstorming webs, task-specific organizers, and thinking-process maps. Each chapter begins with an overview of the form, its purpose, and implications for using the tool for individualized, cooperative, and schoolwide learning. These chapters close with shorter sections that highlight software for using the tool and promising assessment practices. *The sequence of these chapters—brainstorming webs, task-specific organizers, thinking-process maps—should not be construed as a proposed sequence for using these tools in a classroom. I believe there is no such "appropriate" sequence.*

Chapter 6 is an introduction to Thinking Maps, a common language of eight graphically distinct, flexible, and metacognitive visual tools. They are being used in depth in more than 300 whole schools and across entire districts as an interactive, mental toolkit for all students, teachers, and administrators.

The concluding chapter offers a vision of how many of the tools presented in this book offer a way to integrate teaching and learning through *continuous* assessment in classrooms. Final sections of the book provide selected references and resources for teachers as they begin to use visual tools in the classroom.

This integration—this new capacity to see the forest (context) and the trees (details)—is offered as one foundation for school restructuring. It is an effort based on constructivism, student-centered and interactive learning, and new forms of expression that stimulate schools to become continuously self-assessing learning communities.

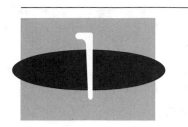

Why Visual Tools Now?

Peek into Norm Schuman's 6th grade social studies classroom in Jackson, Mississippi, and you will see groups of students huddled over books, working together. They are sketching out a picture of information, drawing to the surface essential knowledge that was once bound by text. The students' writings and accompanying maps hang on string that spans the room. The writings and maps also are pinned to display boards in the classroom and hallway, and they are tucked into portfolios in an accessible corner.

Norm Schuman is a highly energetic man, quick with a smile or an idea. Norm might seem to be the kind of teacher who motivates students to learn by his sheer will and endless positive energy. But the truth is, he gives his students assignments that move him quickly to the background. Students have the tools for achieving what he assigns. They are in the foreground, and Norm is the patient sidelines coach.

Today, each of six cooperative learning groups has been asked to read a passage from well-worn texts, on a different Native American tribe. Their task is to identify critical information about each group: customs and celebrations, habitats, foods, gender roles and relationships among members, and spiritual beliefs. Norm emphasizes finding details about each of these topics, along with the fact that he will create the final test questions from the information each group presents.

All groups use a common visual tool—a hierarchical structure—to collect, analyze, and synthesize the text into a clearly defined picture of a tribe. Each group will then share this picture in an oral presentation, using the map as a visual guide on the overhead projector.

Norm methodically moves around the room and looks down at the developing maps, guiding here, scanning there, nodding quietly in agreement at another table. Students' eyes focus intently on their group maps. The groups redraft these maps several times during two periods of instruction until only the most essential ideas have been distilled and organized from the text. In each group, a member takes a colored pen and copies the agreed-upon version onto a transparency page while the other members discuss the rotation they will use for the presentation.

The following day, oral presentations begin. Each group moves to the front of the room, placing a colorful transparency on the overhead. Then each group member speaks about a key point of interest from one area on the map. Their peers are busy at their seats, listening, sketching out the map, and making notes and comparisons to their own work.

Norm is in the back of the room, occasionally reinforcing a certain idea or, when necessary, offering a clarification or correction. But most of the time, Norm asks questions of a higher order. His queries are complex in that each requires students to make inferences from data they have woven together. He asks questions that involve comparisons between tribes. Synthesizing questions require students to construct generalizations; interpretive and predictive queries explore how certain tribes might have reacted to interventions from outside forces. He encourages students in the classroom to ask questions. As each group presents its work, however, Norm jots down new questions he had not thought of in previous years, questions sparked by these student presentations.

Days after the presentations are over, Norm gives the students a test. It includes questions based on text information they presented *and* questions that require them to have linked information from several of the hierarchy maps. He also asks questions that involve the use of other visual tools, such as those for comparing tribes, showing the development of a culture, or explaining the causes and effects of outside interventions. Students are ready for such questions because these tools have become a common way of communicating.

When asked about this process, and especially about the level of his questions—answered by students who have come into his classroom as supposed "underachievers" from low socioeconomic neighborhoods—Norm responds: "I could never have asked these questions of my previous students, most of whom came into my class several years behind in grade-level reading. I didn't give them the tools to make inferences like this. They didn't have the organizational abilities to work with so much information." Norm adds without hesitation that his current students now score higher on his exams than any previous class. Norm smiles, his eyes aglow with a sense of accomplishment: "And I am asking much more complex questions!"

Cave Drawings, Cartography, and Cognition

Visual tools are now becoming key teaching, learning, and assessing tools in many classrooms like Norm Schuman's. Together, students and teachers are generating mental models of how they perceive the world. But why are visual tools growing more popular? The depiction of ideas through visual forms has always been an elemental dimension of human culture. These forms range from cave drawings to perspective drawings, cartography, diagramming of molecular structures, and, most recently, computer-generated flowcharting.

There is no more ready reason for the growing popularity of visual tools than the well-worn social studies textbooks in Norm's class. Students are now faced with an overwhelming, ever-changing *quantity* of data. We are also in the midst of a renaissance in the *quality* of how representations of information and knowledge are represented through different technology— representations that will be transformed anew in the decades to come. Unlike pupils at the turn of the 20th century, students today often work together in cooperative groups with their peers, rather than learn from a lecturing teacher in the solitary confines of bolted-down desks.

Later in this chapter, we explore the following three interrelated reasons for why more and more teachers and students are using visual tools:

• First, we are now teaching and learning in a constructivist-cognitive paradigm.

• Second, new technologies and visual designs are guiding information flow.

• Third, student-centered learning and "interactivity" are emerging as the new structures for classroom relationships.

These three reasons will be continuing focal points as we investigate different types of visual tools and how they are used to integrate teaching, learning, and assessment. But we may better understand these reasons and the visual shift in classrooms by exploring an essential metaphor that explains how these constructivist tools open students' thinking beyond the traditional linear mindset of schooling.

The Map-Making Metaphor

Maps are primary guides in our lives: road maps, world maps, transit and subway diagrams, maps for exploring a museum or amusement park, weather maps, and even imaginary treasure maps. Of course, as we consider geographic knowledge on a map, we see key representations of the essential connections among mountains, valleys, and rivers. Similarly, visual tools are used primarily to make and represent connections among ideas and concepts.

Visual tools offer a bird's-eye view of patterns, interrelationships, and interdependencies. They provide guides for making our way in books full of text or among downloaded materials from the Information Superhighway. Unlike geographic maps, which show explicit *physical* models of the world, visual tools generate and unveil *mental* models of interrelationships developed by learners, along with the unique patterning capacity of each learner's mind. The significant difference between geographic and mental maps is that geographic maps represent relatively static, physical entities, whereas the maps we are investigating represent internal, mental, flexible, often quickly changing, and highly generative patterns.

Visual tools as evolving maps reflect our capacities to pattern and reorganize relationships. The similarity of purpose between geographic and mental maps, moreover, is clear: Each is based on the visual representation of a region, a mental space (Fauconnier 1985) that may be heretofore unknown. Each simultaneously displays a view of both the holistic "forest" and the detailed "trees." Additionally, maps are much like paintings: They are drawn from a certain perspective and thus have limitations. This means that each map is made in the eye of the beholder, with the instruments at hand, and within the intellectual/philosophical paradigm of its maker. This is best illustrated by the continuum in our belief system about our own planet, from the "flat earth" map made by our ancestors to the astronauts' perspective from a valley on the moon.

The unique representations derived from map making are best expressed through the history of cartography, which reveals that this invention was a turning point for human understanding:

> The act of mapping was as profound as the invention of a number system. . . . The combination of the reduction of reality and the construction of an analogical space is an attainment in abstract thinking of a very high order indeed, for it enables one to discover structures that would remain unknown if not mapped (Robinson 1982, p. 1).

This quotation is borrowed from James H. Wandersee's insightful analysis of the connection between cartography and cognition (1990). He suggests that cartography links perception, interpretation, cognitive transformations, and creativity. Wandersee believes that map making serves four basic purposes:

- to challenge one's assumptions,
- to recognize new patterns,
- to make new connections, and
- to visualize the unknown.

The metaphorical relationship between cartography and mental maps of human cognition is useful, though certainly incomplete. *Seeing should not be construed as believing or knowing.* Seeing is one modality for perceiving, though for most of us it is our primary modality. Visual perceptions balance with auditory and kinesthetic access to knowing. Visual tools for mental mapping need to be integrated with other representational and language systems for reflecting different kinds of intelligences (Gardner 1983).

In sum, visual tools are for constructing representations of knowledge. In educational terms, visual tools are for constructing and remembering, communicating and negotiating meanings, and assessing and reforming the shifting terrain of interrelated knowledge. We even use maps to rediscover information, ideas, and experiences lost in the recesses of our minds. We use maps to find our way to new information, much like an evolving treasure map of the mind for seeking new meaning in texts and other materials.

Beyond the Linear Mindset

Unfortunately, in contradiction to the varied and complex patterns generated in our minds, most of the content offered to students is in the representation of linear walls of texts, like the text in the paragraph you just read. Yet students are ultimately responsible for transforming such linear text into multirelational, holistic concepts.

For an extreme example to illustrate this point, consider trying to teach students to understand geographic relationships with written texts *but without geographic maps*. If our minds, and our world of knowledge, are just as or more complex and multidimensional than geographic features, then we often provide representations that do not complement our capacities as learners. In fact, we actually stifle students' thinking

by putting blinders on them, preventing interest in the nonlinear world of ideas. Researchers are finding that the patterning capacity of the human brain is really much closer to the undulating, networked forms of matter we see in the interrelated, physical world:

> All knowledge is "embedded" in other knowledge. . . . The split brain research helped us to appreciate that the brain has an enormous capacity to deal with parts and wholes simultaneously. The brain can deal with the interconnected, interpenetrating, "holographic" world, provided it is encouraged to do so. One common thrust of many new methods of teaching is that they have this sense of "embeddedness" (Caine and Caine 1991).

Traditionally, educators have not encouraged viewing the interconnectedness of knowledge in even the most simplistic sense. Aside from geography lessons, art classes, and geometry, communication in most classrooms is primarily via linear patterns of representation: written (lines of text or mathematical operations) or verbal (people speaking with each other). An occasional timeline, flowchart, Venn diagram, matrix, or axis is used, but it is often relatively static and linear despite its visual form.

Obviously, many students understand concepts as we teach them, but not so obvious is the problem that this understanding may be only from a linear mindset or representational system. Margaret Wheatley suggests:

Our thinking processes have always yielded riches when we've approached things openly, letting free associations form into new ideas. Many would argue that we've used such a small part of our mental capacity because of our insistence on linear thinking (1992, p. 116).

This focus on linear thinking—within a formal framework of hierarchical relationships—is the support system for isolating disciplines and subject areas in schools. Currently, we are going through another wave of integrated and interdisciplinary instructional approaches that encourage students to seek thematic interrelationships. With this new thrust, we also must provide learners with concrete skills, strategies, and tools for seeking out cross-discipline patterns *on their own.*

Deepening this problem even more is that most systems and interdisciplinary themes that we ask students to understand do not act—in reality—within a linear framework. Many systems—like a social system, moral code, ecosystem, solar system, or the human mind-body system—have the qualities of being dynamic, overlapping, elegantly complex, and interrelated. Thus, *if* we want our students to understand and make predictions about interdisciplinary, nonlinear systems, we are not providing the needed tools for them to effectively meet what we and the world expect.

Visual tools, in sum, expand our horizons and refocus our attention, moving us back and forth:

• between auditory/written language and visual representations;

• between linear thinking and holistic, nonlinear thinking;

• between isolated "bits" of facts and patterns and interrelationships; and

• between list-like knowledge and evolving, interdependent systems of learning.

Ultimately, visual tools provide additional constructive linkages between the "inside" holistic mind and body and the "outside" world.

For decades, psychologists, philosophers, and cognitive scientists have aggressively sought better ways of discovering how the mind works and then how it represents that work *process* to the outside world. This research effort, through human and artificial intelligence studies, is ultimately serving educators as we attempt to facilitate students' thinking and learning. If we believe that human perceptions and thought processes are highly interrelated, holistic, and nonlinear—as well as linear—then it makes sense that we have additional nonlinear ways of accessing, interpreting, communicating, and assessing the way we think. This supposition is at the heart of the need for visual tools.

The Need for Visual Tools

The addition of visual tools to ever more inclusive classrooms is showing potential for transforming how ideas, knowledge, dialogue, and meaning are created, communicated, and assessed. Of late, educational leaders have offered many changes for restructuring schools, including how teachers should teach and how all students should learn how to learn. Key to this restructuring effort is the significant pedagogical, political, and funding shift away from tracking students and toward structuring schools with more inclusive, heterogenous classrooms. Educators are moving away from systemic categorization of students and the isolation of many students with special needs, including "special education" and "gifted" students. We are now structuring learning communities that reflect the world of home and work: People with a range of differing learning, cognitive, interpersonal, and communication styles are productively living and working in teams and learning from each other. This dramatic shift requires that teachers acquire new approaches, try new strategies, and offer all students similar resources and intellectual tools for building their intellectual, emotional, and artistic intelligences.

As we shall see in the chapters ahead, some of these new approaches that are drawn from education and business—such as "concept mapping" (Novak and Gowin 1984), Thinking Maps (Hyerle 1995), and systems thinking (Senge 1990)—are directly supported by visual tools. These approaches offer common languages for all students in thinking about, interpreting, and displaying knowledge. These approaches—and other theory-based processes using visual tools—may actually spark a *revolution in representation* in classrooms and in the place where learning is motivated: within the dynamics of the teacher-student relationship.

There are some fairly obvious reasons for this "visual" shift in classrooms. Since the 1950s, our culture has moved from the mechanical into the Information Age, from Newtonian

to quantum physics, from a "hearing" culture into a highly networked, interactive "seeing" culture. Neil Postman has said of this highly paced, accelerating transition that "change changed." From an educator's perspective, this transition has been spurred by at least three interrelated areas:

- the constructivist-cognitive revolution,
- the impact of technology and visual design, and
- the evolution toward student-centered "interactivity."

Together, these "change" areas have established both the platform and necessity for visual tools.

The Constructivist-Cognitive Revolution

Educational historians of future generations will look back on the late 20th century as a time when educators began the slow, institutional transformation away from rote behaviorism, closed definitions of intelligence, and hardened perceptions of a singular, static, "given" structure of knowledge. Initiated in the work of Jean Piaget, the guiding term for this cognitive revolution is *constructivism*.

Early researchers who influenced this direction—such as L.S. Vygotsky in Russia, J.P. Guilford and Benjamin Bloom in the United States, and Reuven Feuerstein in Israel—have supported the last generation of cognitive skills practice in education. Hilda Taba's concept development approach was one of the first significant training programs to translate research into concrete questioning strategies for teachers. This early research and practice influenced the broad-based "thinking skills" movement of the past 20 years, which was led by the works of Arthur Costa, David Perkins, Edward deBono, Matthew Lipman, Richard Paul, and many others (Costa 1985, 1991).

Up to this time, the focal point of education has been slowly shifting from students remembering "bits" of information to students being able to consciously construct conceptual understandings that link the "bits" into patterns of information. The cognitive revolution is based on building students' capacities to integrate knowledge, in marked contrast to a still popular and slowly fading behavioral learning paradigm. The "case for constructivism" has been made:

> Much of traditional education breaks wholes into parts, and then focuses separately on each part. But many students are unable to build concepts and skills from parts to wholes. These students often stop trying to see the wholes before all the parts are presented to them and focus on the small, memorizable aspects of broad units without ever creating the big picture.... We need to see the "whole" before we are able to make sense of the parts (Brooks and Brooks 1993).

The essence of this statement turns on the phrases "build concepts" and "creating the big picture." Though the case for constructivism has been made, these phrases still represent its outposts and unmet expectations, as we are still struggling in a transitional time between paradigms without practical strategies for student-centered construction of knowledge. A shift in paradigms in any field is usually slow; but for several reasons, this shift is difficult for many educators.

Many institutional constraints prevent a shift, including a weak system for translating research into initial training and long-term professional development of teachers; curriculum frameworks grounded almost entirely on scope-and-sequence content learning; and slowly evolving, alternative assessment tools. Of course, the highest hurdle is the historical belief that the purpose of schooling is for the direct transmission of cultural knowledge and scientific, objective truths. In addition, because we don't have many long-term experiments, we also may have to admit that we are still in the discovery phase of learning about how knowledge is actually constructed.

Constructivism is now guided by research in a new area: cognitive science (Gardner 1985). Many educators may be unaware that a variety of researchers, let's call them "neo-Piagetians," have conducted extensive research that questions some of the basic strands of Piaget's stage theory of cognitive development. Starting with Vygotsky's "zone of proximal development," some cognitive scientists have shown that children—given support and scaffolding—are able to construct and understand concepts earlier than once believed. Wide-ranging research in cognitive styles, learning modalities, learning styles, cultural differences, language differences and communication styles across cultures, and, more recently, multiple intelligences has focused on how different people perceive, transform, and convey concepts. Philosophers, anthropologists, linguists, and biologists, as well as researchers of brain functioning and neural "connectionism," have provided foundations from which many new understandings about learning are evolving (Sylwester 1995).

The central problem that constructivist educators face is not a guiding theory, but concrete strategies and tools for institutionalizing these theoretical and practical understandings into more inclusive classrooms. Some constructivist approaches are entering classrooms slowly, such as cooperative learning and conflict resolution, thinking and process writing instruction, integrated and interdisciplinary approaches, and portfolio and performance-based assessment practices. But we are just beginning to articulate how these designs work together. And notice that most of these approaches create the environment for constructivism but do not center explicitly on *how* an individual learner constructs knowledge.

The next chapters of this book explain how visual tools are one avenue for supporting students and teachers in actively connecting information and for discovering interrelated "contents" and "processes." Visual tools are a strong link between teaching content and facilitating and guiding thinking processes. We can begin to see one way of breaking the age-old content/process dichotomy by identifying "forms" or structures of knowledge that bridge this mythical gap.

As we explore in this book, visual tools of many kinds are used to build and then more explicitly express interrelationships, interdepend-

encies, and forms of knowledge. Verbalizing and writing out ideas are only one way of representing thinking, and often this is a thin, linear veneer of students' thinking about content. With visual tools, students begin to visually integrate their own holistic forms with the tightly wound structures of information and thus interpret text. They begin to identify and then integrate their forms with the text as they naturally link information. Visual brainstorming webs, task-specific organizers, and thinking-process maps thus provide a bridge between their own forms and the structures that are embodied in the text but hidden in the guise of linear strings of words.

The Impact of Technology and Visual Design

Some 50 years after the first televisions took center stage, the Information Age has blossomed through new technologies that are especially visual. Videocassette recorders and video cameras are commonplace; computer screens illuminate most businesses, some homes, and many schools and classrooms; CD-ROM technology offers a new degree of accessibility to visually supported information.

Of course, the computer is much more than a new television console to huddle around and *watch*. We are guided and also required to make decisions, seek, and invent—and these actions are becoming ever more compatible with, and facilitative of, our natural thinking processes. We now have a different reflection of ourselves. As Margaret Wheatley observes, "Now we have the technology to mirror more generative processes. More and more, the world of information is associative, networked, and heuristic" (1992, p. 117).

As Wheatley suggests, one of the exciting qualities of the computer is that it may be used as a metacognitive tool, an electronic reflecting pool for the mind. New technologies have usually given us innovative ways to investigate and understand our world and ourselves. If we are humble and philosophical, we realize that these technologies may also reveal to us how much we still do not understand about the world or our own thinking. The empowering effect of the computer is that its capacity is partly a projection (or simplistic reflection) of the neural networking of our minds. Given this capacity, it is hardly a coincidence that the mid-1950s saw a parallel growth of knowledge about both human and computer intelligence. Researchers showed increased interest in facilitating students' thinking and in fostering human intelligence at the same time that computer research spread into artificial intelligence.

The invention of the computer is a mixed blessing for educators, because we now face a new kind of student. This new student, on average, spends more time in childhood in front of a television or computer screen than in a classroom. Some novice adult computer users are just learning how to get onto the Information Superhighway, dodging high-speed information blocks and wondering what to do with all of the information available. Many students see this kind of access as exciting and fun, not as a dilemma. Where they are intrigued by the endless playfulness of computers, most adults are playing catch-up. At the same time, educators are

witnessing the "overstimulation" of students who have too much information and few intellectual tools to evaluate the multitude of data available to them.

This excess of information is leading to a growing consensus in educational communities. We must catch up quickly and begin to integrate computers and quality software into schools so that computer-literate students are skillful, reflective, mindful users of information, or "infotectives":

> Unless students have a toolkit of thinking and problem-solving skills which match the feasts of information so readily available, they may emerge from their meal bloated with techno-garbage, information junk food. . . . We must guide our students to become infotectives. What is an infotective? . . . [It is a] student thinker capable of asking great questions about data (with analysis) in order to convert the data into information (data organized so as to reveal patterns and relationships) and eventually into insight (information which may suggest action or strategy of some kind) (McKenzie 1996).

It is clear from this view that students need new tools for organizing and analyzing information provided through visual technology. How? By seeking relevant patterns and relationships and thereby more easily discarding irrelevant masses of data.

An essential problem facing educators is how the information overflow is represented, accessed, and then controlled by students. This new problem is based in the visual design of information. Whereas televisions of old provided an unchangeable screen, the visual screens of computers and innovative television technologies are our students' new visual screen. This colorful, dynamic screen is a mental space based in graphical representations linking infinite interrelationships. But it is also a place where students can become overwhelmed by information and mostly entertained by multimedia bytes.

Given the entertaining and motivating factors of computer use, how information is represented is of utmost concern. The structure and *design* of information is critical, because we can also be so easily deceived or overrun by what we see. Edward Tufte, in his illustrative text *Envisioning Information* (1990), presents the essential attributes of high-quality information design in charts, graphs, tables, and other visual representations. As Tufte relates, we live in "information-thick worlds," not because of computers but because of our human capacities to create complex designs. These designs are evermore dependent upon integrated, nonlinear, visual representations. He states:

> Visual displays rich with data are not only an appropriate and proper complement to human capacities, but also such designs are frequently optimal. If the visual task is contrast, comparison, and choice—as so often it is—then the more relevant information within eyespan, the better (Tufte 1990).

The key to quality information design is found in the efforts for what Tufte calls "escaping flatlands": the bland, tabulated masses of predigested or raw data portrayed in lines of data on the screen. Effective and efficient visual displays are borne of the necessity to escape the endless flatlands. This image is best told by Tufte's description of a computer-graphical timetable used for the high-speed Tokyo train system, which balances the use of computers with graphic displays on paper:

> The Tokyo control-room directing these high-speed trains is filled with these graphical timetables, long paper strips used to help oversee thousands of journeys each day—a task which makes clear the enormous advantages of seeing information rather than tabulating data (Tufte 1990).

The computer as an information delivery system and organizing tool has evolved in complexity in dynamic relationship to the tasks of our modern technologies. As with the previous example, however, little of the *thinking* about information happens inside a computer.

Although the computer environment may affect thought patterns, thinking happens in the mind of the learner. Like a director in the Tokyo control room, today's student (as a future Information Age worker) needs visual organizing tools for sorting out, evaluating, displaying, and making decisions about information. Throughout their school lives, students must be able to practice and improve their capacities to gain control over the actual patterning of information. Some educators believe that asking higher-order questions of students and guiding them to ask these questions of themselves will solve this problem.

Unfortunately, facilitating students' abilities to ask insightful questions is not going to be enough. Students also need tools they can use to fully investigate such questions. Students need to be able to know how to access and consciously transform information.

Student-Centered Interactivity

The expectations and needs of the constructivist-cognitive revolution and the new visual technologies for accessing and displaying information are interrelated within schools' much broader movement toward student-centered interaction, cooperative learning, and interactivity.

Before leaving the subject of technology and turning to the needs of visual tools for cooperative learning, let's investigate a key term in the field of technology: *interactivity.* Remember the interactive, seemingly personable and caring computer named Hal in the movie *2001, A Space Odyssey?* Hal converses in a personable way with the pilot Dave. Hal thinks through problems and eventually takes over the controls of the spaceship. Though this scenario is certainly fiction, it is also scientifically real. We are moving toward more open, interactive learning communities, and computers are part of the conversation. In the field of technology, this dimension is called interactivity. Soon, students will have greater capacities to communicate and interact with the computer as an intelligent technology and with other computer users. But what is interactivity?

On one level, interactivity is the student's access to driving the learning experience. Tom Snyder, creator of some of the most challenging, provocative, and interactive technologies available, discusses the connections among interactions between student and machine, in linear and nonlinear forms:

> In the computer world, "linear" implies not branching, which is not entirely desirable because computers can be highly nonlinear in the way they work. At a branch in a computer circuit, for example, you can make one choice to go one way and another choice to go another—that's what a computer does well. Branching is at the heart of hypertext. In hypertext, you create your own path through a book. Instead of starting at the beginning and working your way methodically through to the end, you create your own knowledge and your own understanding based on the way you learn and what you need and what you think. Hypertext, the book of the future, is totally interactive in this way (Snyder 1994).

Although you might disagree that hypertext will be the "book of the future," the visual flatland of the computer screen and multimedia approaches to information are forcing us to build students' capabilities to make their own pathways and create their own knowledge. Within these processes, students are interacting with computers and with other "infotectives." Ultimately, many of our students will interact in real time with peers who are not in their own classroom, or even on the same continent. Thus, technologies of this age are propelling many teachers into a new view of learning:

from teacher-centered lecture to student-centered interactivity.

In schools throughout the United States, cooperative learning and conflict resolution are changing the dynamics of classrooms and whole learning communities. Cooperative learning provides active roles for students as they work together, with coaching from teachers. Conflict resolution is based on processes, skills, and interpersonal communication strategies that students learn to use to manage interpersonal conflicts. In addition, many schools have well-trained student mediators who facilitate conflicts between students. A core value of these approaches—returning to John Dewey—is nestled within a belief that students should be interactive learners who connect their experiences in the world to the learning context and reflect on processes and behaviors. This is in contrast to being passive recipients of teacher-, text-, or computer-driven information and processes.

These capacities for student-centered, interactive learning are similar to the key goals of thinking-process instruction: a focus on teachers facilitating independent learning; students becoming aware of commonly shared learning processes; students becoming fluent in articulating their ideas and values as interdependent participants in the classroom; and students independently and consciously transferring "learning how to learn" skills to other environments, including the workplace.

With this shift toward interactive learning and interactivity, there is a need for a range of different *student-centered* tools for basic communication and learning. Why? As a teacher takes

on different roles in the classroom (coach, guide, facilitator, source of knowledge), students are asked to take greater responsibility for their own intellectual and interpersonal work. Therefore, collaborative strategies and tools are needed to provide some of the glue that holds a group together, a responsibility that heretofore has been carried almost exclusively by teachers and administrators.

This need for collaborative tools is a central theme of the remainder of this book, because visual tools make ideas public, accessible, and shared in cooperative learning groups. The advantages for using visual learning tools are different depending on the type of tool being used, which the next chapters discuss in context.

The changes in student-teacher interactions and student-to-computer interactivity also require new strategies and tools for communication that can be used throughout a school or business. Ultimately, this need is felt most concretely as students make the school-to-work transition. Today's students will regularly move in and out of jobs that require the capacities for information processing, group problem solving, and interpersonal skills. As these workers face the prospect of changing jobs frequently, they will need the capacities and tools for continuous learning and self-assessment—and for communicating their ideas within different groups of people and organizations. Today's students will be responsible for seeking different views of information and negotiating these viewpoints. They need to become responsible members of culturally diverse working groups gathered from within the United States and around the world.

* * *

We are only at the beginning of integrating visual tools into learning environments in both schools and businesses. It is becoming clear that what learners are thinking *and* how they express their thinking will be the central concerns of this shift. On a deeper level, the more visual tools are used to express ideas, the more there also may be a shift in how we actually define things. Traditionally, we isolate knowledge to define "things." Given visual tools, learners are motivated to seek definitions that are relational, patterned, and context-driven. This means that the basis for *definitions* may change:

> This world of relationships is rich and complex. Gregory Bateson (1980) speaks of "the pattern that connects," and urges that we stop teaching facts— the "things" of knowledge—and focus,

instead, on relationships as the basis for all definitions (Wheatley 1992).

Though few educators would support a radical movement away from teaching "facts," most believe that the ultimate goal of education is not about students' memorizing facts. Students must be able to demonstrate that they can create concepts from related "facts." Importantly, both the forest (patterns and context) and the trees (detailed information) need to remain within view. The focus of future teaching, learning, and assessing will not be remembering only isolated "things" but on how students interactively construct "the pattern that connects."

We now turn to the next link in our investigation, a chapter that provides a definition for different types of visual tools and key questions that educators face in bringing visual tools into schools.

*

Introducing Visual Tools

The exciting variety of visual tools now used in classrooms has also brought about a confusion of terms and definitions. The following terms are often used synonymously: webs, mindmaps, spider maps, clusters, semantic maps, concept maps, cognitive maps, graphic organizers, and—more recently—Thinking Maps and systems thinking feedback diagramming.

Some educators, saturated with brainstorming webs during professional development workshops or the graphics presented in textbooks, may look at new visual tools and say "Oh, we've done that before." This attitude is quite understandable because on first glance, many of these visual forms *look* like any other. But the distinctions among different visual tools can be profound. The true definition of each visual tool is usually found in how it is explained and introduced to students and its subsequent *interactive use*—not in how it *looks*.

This chapter offers an introduction to visual tools, a summary of the successes of these forms across disciplines, a definition of and metaphor for the use of visual tools, and a brief description of three types of tools. These sections are followed by practical concerns and questions about how to introduce visual tools into a classroom or whole school. This includes steps for reviewing visual tools in your learning environment, how to introduce the tools to students, guiding questions for choosing appropriate tools, and an overview for using visual tools in cooperative learning.

The questions raised in this chapter are offered as guides to active reading of the remainder of the book. Thus, this chapter is a taking-off point for a deeper discussion and more comprehensive view of each of the three types of visual tools we explore.

Cross-Discipline Successes

One of the reasons for bringing some clarity and definition to different types of visual tools is that their long-term potential and significance may be eroded if students, teachers, and administrators—along with publishers and researchers—do not begin a discussion of their common benefits and best uses. These tools are being used successfully and differently across disciplines, deepening content-specific and interdisciplinary understandings, but mostly they are used in isolated situations. We find few instances of consistent and coordinated use of these tools over multiple years of schooling.

For example, in the field of science, students may use hierarchical "concept mapping" to develop visual mental models of how they perceive scientific concepts. Teachers use those mental models to assess the development of students' concepts and misconceptions. Teachers of mathematics, having long ago added to the

Venn diagram, have become leaders in promoting students' use of visual modeling such as flowcharting and diagrams for problem solving and concept development. For reading comprehension across disciplines, students practice with visual scaffolds—text structures—to analyze and synthesize meaningful patterns of ideas not readily apparent in page after page of text. And, increasingly, brainstorming webs, or "mindmapping," have become basics in many schools for writing process instruction. Finally, with the rise of the thinking skills movement, we have seen extensive use of maps based on thinking processes, enabling students to transfer complex thinking skills in the form of tools across disciplines. Though the uses of these tools overlap, there is rarely a coordinated effort to help students make sense of all of them.

Of course, successes with these tools are happening without coordination, but even a limited effort in a school or district to identify, share best uses, and agree on some common visual tools could exponentially expand their quality use by students. Extensive qualitative evidence and standardized test results show that these tools change student performance. Some of the test results are presented as we explore different types of visual tools in the following chapters. The qualitative results accumulated over the years from teachers, students, and researchers alone reveal that visual tools are enhancing students':

- motivation to learn;
- basic skills of reading, writing, and arithmetic;
- content knowledge retention;

- general communication skills;
- organizing abilities;
- independent and cooperative learning;
- problem-solving flexibility;
- creative and analytical thinking;
- conceptual understandings;
- higher-order thinking;
- metacognitive abilities and self-assessment; and
- enjoyment of problem solving.

The last item in this list is linked directly to the first: Students are motivated to learn when they enjoy the process. A nearly universal response from teachers who have experimented with visual tools reveals an often undervalued and ungraded change in performance: enjoyment of an intellectual challenge.

There is also great potential for the use of these tools for students with special needs, especially when all students in a classroom and school are using common visual tools. Students are motivated by using tools for actively and visually *constructing* "whole" ideas independently and in cooperative learning groups. The use of visual tools creates a shift in classroom dynamics from passive to active and interactive learning for all to see.

Defining Visual Tools

Historically, the most commonly used name for visual tools has been either *semantic maps* or, more recently, *graphic organizers*. A succinct definition of graphic organizers is found in one of the most comprehensive theoretical and practical investigations of these tools, a text written

by John Clarke entitled *Patterns of Thinking*. This text is required reading for educators interested in studying a comprehensive research base on visual tools. Clarke defines graphic organizers as:

> [Words] on paper, arranged to represent an individual's understanding of the relationship between words. Whereas conventions of sentence structure make most writing linear in form, graphic organizers take their form from the presumed structure of relationships among ideas (1991, p. 30).

Whereas this definition clearly and simply expresses the open, generative quality of some graphic forms, the term *organizer* may not fully represent the many different types and uses of these tools. The implication of that term is that these graphics are used *only* for organizing information. Yet many visual tools that might be called "graphic organizers" are used for brainstorming, seeking open-ended associations, and consciously delaying organization. Other visual tools have been designed for moving well beyond brainstorming and organizing ideas to specifically facilitate dialogue, perspective taking, mediation of student thinking, metacognition, theory development, and self-assessment.

Unfortunately, the worst-case scenario for the use of "graphic organizers" (called "task-specific organizers" in this book) is when students repetitively use preformed organization charts as merely "fill-in" boxes on activity sheets. Several publishers offer packets of fill-in graphic forms that have extremely limited and intellectually limiting use. These activities, while helpful in some special cases, are not too far removed from students' filling in empty spaces on worksheets, a commonplace activity ever since the creation of workbooks, blackline masters, and duplicating machines.

Another term, *semantic maps*, has also been used to represent the field of visual tools. But historically, the term has been used predominantly for describing brainstorming webs for writing process and language arts instruction. Visual tools are now used well beyond the field of semantics.

Neither graphic organizer nor semantic maps satisfactorily represents the dynamic quality and wide range of uses that the phrase *visual tools* offers. The term *tool* conveys the essential quality of these visuals: They are dynamic and constructive in the hands of students. The following expanded definition for visual tools is a synthesis of John Clarke's (1991) definition for graphic organizers and many of the ideas that will be investigated throughout this book.

> Visual tools are symbols graphically linked by mental associations to create a pattern of information and a form of knowledge about an idea. These linear or nonlinear forms are constructed by individual or collaborative thinkers on paper, board, or computer screen.
>
> There are three basic types of visual tools: brainstorming webs, task-specific organizers, and thinking-process maps. Though each of these types of visual tools may be defined for a specific purpose or used together, each form also may require the use of one or several different global processes, including generating, analyzing, organizing, synthesizing, and evaluating meanings.

Using the term *tool* is crucial to this definition, and clarifies what *is not* being investigated in this book. There are many valuable graphic representations that are used primarily for storing, graphing, or displaying information, often after much of the thinking about a problem has been completed. These forms include matrix diagrams, tables, basic charts, axis diagrams, bar graphs, and pie diagrams. These types of graphics may be used for analysis and to facilitate evaluation and other complex tasks. But they are often used as *place-holders* and displays for information and not specifically as constructive *tools*.

Theory-Embedded Tools

One way to think about the tool-like quality of these representations is to consider an underlying metaphor for the idea of a tool. The meaning of the term *tool* as used here comes from the philosophical and psychological stance of constructivism, which is based on several metaphors. One central metaphor is that of a student building knowledge, much like a carpenter building a house with materials such as wood, nails, concrete, and glass. These are the contents of the work. A carpenter comes to a job with the practical abilities to mold and structure these materials. Those abilities—both discrete skills and general strategies—have been learned through years of experience at different jobs. At most work sites, carpenters apprentice and work in teams while being guided and supervised by a mentor who is a knowledgeable, expert, responsible, licensed contractor.

One of the first things that a carpenter does upon arrival at the work site is to put on a tool belt that holds a hammer, screwdriver, tape measure, and other necessary tools. These are the basics of the trade, skillfully used to directly form materials and construct a final product. So too, a student entering the classroom needs a "tool belt" of sorts, filled with a variety of visual tools that are well defined, developmentally appropriate, and flexibly used to construct meanings.

By way of the development, definition, and use of a visual tool, each *explicitly* embodies one or several processes, just as a hammer explicitly embodies the process of hammering. This explicitness of process, in turn, implies an underlying theory for the tool, or what have been called "theory-embedded tools" (McTighe and Lyman 1988). In their introduction to several different kinds of learning tools, including what they call "cognitive maps," McTighe and Lyman draw from the research of Nathanial Gage (1974), who proposed four requirements for teaching/learning tools. Each tool should have:

- *psychological validity*—it reflects what is known about teaching and learning;
- *concreteness*—it embodies knowledge in materials and equipment;
- *relevance to teachers*—it has practical value in the classroom;
- *differentiation by type of learning*—a relationship exists between the type of tool and the way that a skill, concept, process, or attitude is best learned.

This set of four attributes creates a helpful filter for thinking about the difference between a visual tool and content knowledge as well as the difference between a visual tool and a skill or process.

Using this filter, the visual tools investigated in this book are:

- *psychologically valid* given our present knowledge about the processes of teaching and learning, especially schema theory, various learning theories, and brain research;
- *concretely* linked to how knowledge is formed, because they tangibly represent and thus embody this knowledge;
- *relevant for teachers* because students are able to use the tools on a daily basis to learn content and improve thinking processes;
- *differentiated* by way of the various types of visual tools that relate directly to different ways of perceiving, conceiving of, and patterning knowledge.

So what is the difference between a tool and a skill or a strategy? Visual tools are neither contents nor processes; they are tools of the learner's trade for concretely *forming* knowledge. Specifically, visual tools are not, in and of themselves, skills or strategies, in the same way that one does not say that a hammer, saw, or screwdriver is a carpentry "skill." A visual tool is a concrete extension and application of one or several skills. It takes a skillful hand to use a jigsaw to cut a delicate pattern in wood, just as it takes a skillful thinker to create a multidirectional feedback flowchart of an ecosystem. Thus, visual tools are *instruments* used skillfully and strategically by teachers and students to construct content knowledge.

Types of Visual Tools

We could categorize examples of visual tools in many ways: how they are used, the rules for constructing the graphic, degree of flexibility in use, the theoretical foundation, and, more practically, how each approach is integrated into classroom use for specific objectives. The categories established for this book are based on concrete, practical purposes: The form of the visual tool often follows its function.

The three relatively distinct yet sometimes overlapping purposes of these tools are, respectively, for brainstorming, task-specific organization of information, and to transfer thinking processes across disciplines. The Tree Map in Figure 2.1 shows the three types of visual tools and examples of each.

Interestingly, each of the three purposes easily could be construed to reflect certain philosophies of educating:

- brainstorming for fostering individual and group creativity,
- task-specific organizers for fostering basic skills and deep content learning, and
- thinking-process maps for fostering cognitive development and critical thinking.

These philosophical points will come into focus in the following three chapters.

These categories are offered as a way of distinguishing these tools so each type may be used with greater clarity and purpose—and used together when it is appropriate for the classroom activities. Several of the developers of the examples described in the following three chapters might argue that their ultimate goal is for their graphic to be used to support two or all three of these purposes. This may be a valid criticism of this category structure, since most categories have "fuzzy" boundaries. Keep in mind, then, that these categories were constructed so as not to be mutually exclusive. In addition, there is absolutely no "most appropriate" sequence of hierarchical design for using these tools. A student may begin a learning activity by using a task-specific organizer, shift to a brainstorming web, and finally focus by using a thinking-process map.

Before looking at each of these types of tools, it is important that educators consider their own learning environment and past experiences to identify visual tools that are already being used. It is also essential, before this discussion, for practitioners to consider some essential questions about, and suggestions for, using tools:

- How do I introduce visual tools to students?
- How do I choose appropriate tools?
- How are these tools used with cooperative learning?

These concerns, questions, and suggestions provide a framework for exploring the remainder of this book.

Reviewing Your Toolkit

The first step in introducing visual tools into a classroom or whole school is to identify those situations where visual tools are already being used. Take these experiences and successes as the starting point for both expanding the repertoire of tools and for focusing more

Tree Map Showing Types of Visual Tools

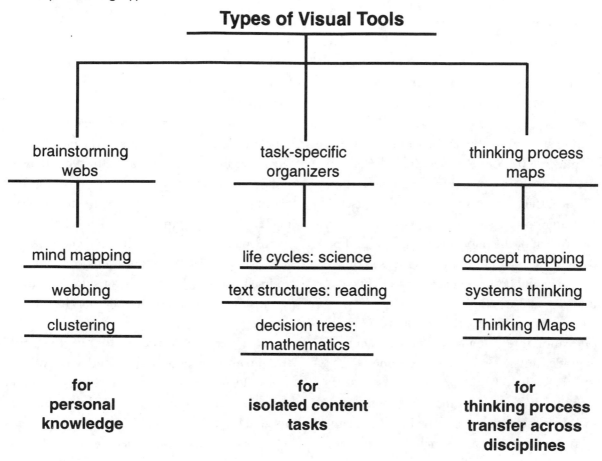

deeply on tools you have found or believe to be successful. This kind of analysis and collection of examples will support you through this reading. Consider this set of reflective questions:

• How do you already use visual tools or other graphics such as charts, pie diagrams, Venn diagrams, flowcharts?

Which of these are most successful? Why?

• If you and your colleagues are already using visual tools, what type are you using (brainstorming webs, task-specific organizers, thinking-process maps)? Are you using one type more than another? Why?

• Do your students enjoy using these tools? Are the tools being used in paired and cooperative learning settings? Ask your students: "How are these visual tools helping you learn?"

- Are students learning to use visual tools on their own and in flexible ways and for interdisciplinary learning? Can students use these tools without your guidance?

- Is there any common use of the same visual tools across the whole school? Is the lack of consistency in the use of visual tools from previous classes confusing your students?

- What are the types of visual tools suggested in student textbooks? Are these tools used meaningfully, or are these just add-on activities? Is there consistency in the definition and use of the tool, or is the same visual used for different processes?

- Which of the published materials and professional development resources focused on visual tools would best support your students, classroom, and whole school?

- Has your district, county, or state office of education integrated visual tools into curriculum guides and assessment instruments?

Embedded in each of these questions are some obvious assumptions. The issues brought up through these questions include the use of visual tools: breadth in the type and number, interactiveness, flexibility, consistency, independence, meaningfulness, and integration with assessment.

As we investigate different types of visual tools, these issues will come to the surface. Though there are no absolute answers to these questions, there are some commonsense responses and research showing the best practices in classrooms and whole schools.

Choosing Appropriate Visual Tools

The pleasurable dilemma of choosing the most appropriate tool becomes more interesting as a classroom adds more tools to its intellectual toolkit. But this is only a short-term problem as students practice and become fluent with each new form.

Choosing the appropriate visual tool, or a set of visual tools, compares to the challenge a carpenter faces when considering what to use to build a structure. The carpenter must first think about the need for a tool as related to the ultimate objective or outcome—what is being built. As we look ahead to the following chapters, here are some essential questions you may ask yourself and suggestions to consider as you think about introducing visual tools to students:

1. Which type of visual tool best supports the purpose or learning objective of this study? Identifying the purpose of an activity and the expectations for students is key to choosing a visual tool. For example, if you want students to generate ideas for a project or piece of writing, a brainstorming web may be used. If you want students to organize information in a highly specific way, such as a defined order of operations for solving an equation, then a task-specific organizer may work. And, if you want students to independently apply a thinking process such as comparison to a reading selection about two characters, then a thinking-process map will fit the need. As mentioned previously, there is no generalizable sequence for using visual tools.

2. What form of the tool is developmentally appropriate? Once you have clarified the visual tool(s) that fit your purpose, you will need to consider the form of the tool. For lower elementary students, the graphic must be large enough to draw pictures, and instructions must be given verbally. Coloring crayons and pens also will help give form to these graphics. The fewer types of visual forms (circles, rectangles, triangles) the better for all elementary students. Highly complex and densely packed visual tools lose their usefulness at any level. For upper elementary and secondary students, clear guidance in the reason and steps for using the visual tools independently is important so that students make meaningful use of the tool.

3. How will we—as a class—interactively use this tool? It is important to decide how the tool will be used: individually, in pairs, and in cooperative groups? As a whole class through teacher direction and facilitation? Or a combination of the above, such as the use of the Think-Pair-Share format?

4. How will we assess the effectiveness of this tool? After you and your students have practiced using a visual tool, it is important to reflect on its usefulness. You and your students must evaluate whether or not, and how, the tool furthered learning and thinking.

5. Is this tool going to be used throughout the year and in coordination with other visual tools? If you are committed to using particular visual tools consistently throughout the year, the processes by which the tool is introduced, improved, and integrated into teaching,

learning, and assessment is important. If you take this step, you are telling students that you want them to gain ownership of the tool so they will use it independently. Make this clear to students by telling them that you want them to take control of their own learning by using the tool regularly, without prompting.

The Importance of Student Ownership of Visual Tools

> Give students worksheets and they will learn for today; teach students how to use a visual tool and they will learn for a lifetime.

One of the most common areas of agreement among those who have used visual tools is that what distinguishes them from static graphic displays is that students use them to become independent, flexible, and interdependent builders of knowledge. As students gain ownership of these tools for active meaning making, the experience is intrinsically rewarding.

As you read the chapters ahead, consider how you might introduce visual tools to students so that they become fluent with graphically representing their ideas. If you want students to gain full ownership of a tool, some form of a systematic introduction is necessary, followed by modeling, practice, and coaching.

The following sequence of steps for introducing a visual tool was provided in an article about using task-specific organizers for reading comprehension across disciplines. This process works well for a graphic in any content area:

> 1. Present at least one good example of a completed graphic outline.
>
> 2. Model how to construct either the same graphic outline or the one to be introduced.
>
> 3. Provide procedural knowledge.
>
> 4. Coach the students.
>
> 5. Give the students opportunities to practice (Jones, Pierce, and Hunter 1988/1989, p. 24).

Notice that Jones et al. are not describing a "graphic organizer" that is printed on a page for students to work through or fill in, as with a worksheet. Initially, students are learning how to draw, change, expand, and manipulate a visual tool so that they construct knowledge on their own in response to the structure of the text or other learning resources. Students should also be asked to review, reflect on, and assess their evolving capacities to use visual tools.

The example provided in Figure 2.2 shows how a 4th grade teacher might introduce a task-specific organizer to students over several days. The task, common from kindergarten through college literature courses, requires students to examine the rising action of a story as a specific dimension of plot analysis. The Rising Action Organizer is first introduced using a story students have already finished reading. Notice the focus during the procedures, coaching, and practice steps. It is on students being able to use the tools individually, in cooperative pairs and groups, and for homework. Students also are asked to use the organizer for verbalizing how they perceive the pattern of information and to compare interpretations.

Some adaptations of this process are made for lower elementary students. For example, teachers may first want to distribute a pre-drawn organizer to all students and have them draw pictures and write a few words in each box. The task vocabulary will no doubt be simplified to "beginning, middle, and end" rather than "rising action, climax, and denouement." In addition, the modeling stage of introduction may go on for several weeks before students— even kindergartners—begin drawing their own boxes and start down the road to independent use of visual tools.

Once this visual tool is fully introduced to students, what does the change mean for teachers? First, students have a concrete way of seeing the key relationships built into the task and directly linked with related vocabulary (in this case, rising action, climax, ending or denouement). Second, as students use the tool, teachers are able to assess their view of the pattern of the story efficiently and effectively by viewing the completed organizers. In a typical classroom without visual tools, a teacher is often dependent upon direct questioning or written responses by students. Most of the time, teachers will have time for only one or two students to respond. Third, discussion and dialogue between students is supported because students have their visual representation displayed in front of them and thus can visually and verbally share their ideas. Fourth, the teacher can facilitate a discussion using the same graphic on the chalkboard or overhead projector.

FIGURE 2.2

Introducing a Visual Tool: Task-Specific Organizer—"Rising Action"

Purpose: Use the "Rising Action" organization for identifying and analyzing the significant events leading up to the climax of a story and ending (or denouement).

1. Example: Distribute this completed example of the organizer, using a story students have recently read.

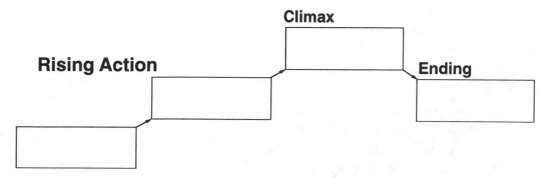

Introduce the vocabulary for each box (important events, climax, ending) and state the purpose for using the organizers and how this tool will help students organize the plot of a story in a meaningful way.

2. Modeling: Read a new story with students, and ask them to think about this organizer as they read. After completion of the story, slowly create the "Rising Action" organizer on the chalkboard without student input. Start with the climax "box," explaining your interpretation of the climax of the story. (This models your metacognitive processes with the tool.) Then proceed to show and explain the rising action of events and ending. Ask for clarifying questions.

3. Procedures: After completion of the modeling, ask students to create a "Rising Action" organizer on a sheet of paper. Have students draw their own organizers so that they immediately take responsibility for using and owning the tool. Discuss the need for starting at the top, using only rectangles, and linking the literature-based vocabulary to the visual tool. Discuss possible variations, such as adding more boxes, if necessary.

4. Coaching: On the next day, ask students to read a new story and structure students in a "Think-Pair-Share" format for creating a "Rising Action" organizer. As the pairs are constructing the organizers, move around the classroom and coach students as they work. Ask several pairs of students to share their organizers with the class and discuss the different interpretations and how they have used the tool.

5. Practice: Reinforce the use of the organizer with each reading selection. Assign the organizer for homework so that students have time to practice on their own.

6. Reflection: Ask students to discuss the effectiveness of the visual tool and how this tool could be used in other subject areas, such as in history.

Finally, once students learn how to use a visual tool, the teacher and students save the most precious resource of any given school day: *time*. Time is saved in three basic ways:

• First, students are able to do more independent, meaningful work, enabling the teacher to spend less time explaining terms and concepts.

• Second, during instruction, teachers may quickly assess students' patterns of thinking about content, thus enabling more effective, focused instruction.

• Third, over the school year, more formal assessment is supported as students collect samples of applications in a portfolio that provides the teacher with an effective, time-saving way to review individual growth and group progress.

Possibly the greatest area of time saving is in this area of assessment. Visual tools provide teachers with a picture of student thinking—the same display that students can use for self-assessment. One of the main reasons that we have difficultly assessing students is not because we don't realize the depth and importance of the task; rather, it is because the task is extremely time-consuming and students' verbal or written abilities may not match their thinking abilities. As we look at different visual tools, it will become clear that each form has unique dimensions that foster effective and deep levels of reflectiveness and self-assessment.

Constructing Knowledge in Cooperative Groups

A last area to consider before looking closely at different types of visual tools is their effectiveness for cooperative learning, or, more specifically, how these tools facilitate the sharing and building of knowledge in a group setting. Within each of the next three chapters there will be sections devoted to the use of visual tools for individual, cooperative, and school-wide learning. Following is a brief summary of the implications for using visual tools in an interactive, inclusive classroom that constantly shifts among individual, paired, cooperative, and whole-class learning structures.

Individual Sharing

Given visual tools, students can individually generate ideas apart from the group and then share their ideas. This action promotes visual dialogue: students have the means to convey the holism of their thinking to peers rather than rely exclusively on linear speech or writing. For those students who are not strong at verbalizing their ideas, visual tools become the platform from which they can more fully express their thinking in a paired problem-solving format or group setting. Visual tools also provide a safe haven for every student—across all ability levels for a certain task—to generate and show their thinking.

Negotiating Meanings

In pairs or cooperative learning groups, students use visual tools for negotiating meanings (Novak and Gowin 1984) and not merely mimicking existing knowledge provided by the teacher. Visual tools become a vehicle for deepening and expressing individual views of how information is connected, for sharing multiple perspectives and opinions, and for rigorously discussing different cultural frames of reference. It is much easier for a peer group, or a single dominant voice, to dismiss alternative points of view that are stated in a few sentences than a visual display of interconnected ideas supporting a different perspective. In an inclusive classroom, all students can share their ideas with others, incorporating new information from other students' maps, while developing their own understandings of contents and processes.

Staying Focused

As the old saying goes, talk is cheap, and this can be particularly true in some cooperative learning groups where students stray from the task at hand. Visual tools give students alternative, concrete structures for focusing and persevering in long work sessions, for extensive interdisciplinary projects, and for working together with information as they form a final product.

Teacher Facilitation of Groups

Teachers may support and guide the construction of knowledge in the group by suggesting certain tools that may be most helpful. This may be followed by the teacher's moving around from table to table, *seeing* the progressing ideas and offering reflective questions and coaching. This also enables the teacher to review the group's work with much less intrusion than required when interrupting to ask how things are progressing.

Group Presentations

Students are often asked to make group presentations of ideas to classmates. If everyone in the class has access to common visual tools,

an oral presentation supported by such visuals means that a classroom discussion or dialogue may be richer. This is because the organization of the main and supporting ideas is available for all to see and interpret, shown in the example of Norm Schuman's classroom presented at the beginning of Chapter 1.

Group Self-Assessment

Once a view of knowledge has been constructed in the group, students may look down on the map of their work and be able to evaluate both the holistic view of their understanding and the supporting connections. As different groups present their constructed views of knowledge, students and teachers alike are able to compare alternative structures that have been created and thus evaluate with greater depth not only the product of learning but also the otherwise hidden processes and forms of knowing.

Beyond Blueprints

Teachers, curriculum authors, and test creators face an essential question: Who holds the blueprint for knowledge? Consider carpenters, who work together with a blueprint for a structure that is given to them by the contractor. During the construction process, the carpenters may choose to use certain techniques and make minor changes in detailing, but each carpenter is constructing a building with a *predetermined outcome*. For most carpenters this is not a problem, but the issue of outcomes remains a conundrum in the teacher-student relationship.

As curriculum standards are tightened—and standardized tests remain important—the quality and use of visual tools forces the issue of outcomes to the surface. Many visual tools, by definition, embody the value of students actively constructing knowledge and building theory. This highlights an unresolved problem of constructivism: Are educators interested in giving students their own tools for critically analyzing accepted "truths" and for constructing new knowledge, or are we only giving students enough skills and tools to "frame" knowledge within the boundaries of old paradigms?

Visual tools provide only one of many answers to this dilemma. By learning and using a visual tool, students are given the opportunity and responsibility to actively construct and show how they perceive ideas. Teachers who use visual tools are explicitly showing the relationships that they deem essential for learning. Together, teachers and students are able to use visual tools to actively compare and negotiate meanings they espouse in the classroom in a clear, holistic way. The process of this negotiation is the heart of the educational experience.

These issues are addressed in the next chapters as we look closely at three different types of tools. As you continue reading, consider that, in fact, visual tools are not blueprints for students to follow, but the tools that they can use for the construction of knowledge.

Brainstorming Webs

I n the late 1930s, Alex Osborn initiated the first visual brainstorming sessions in his advertising company. He later wrote a text outlining rules for the group process, which included making no judgments, welcoming "wildness," eliciting quantity, and seeking improvement (Wycoff 1991). Today, the focused use of brainstorming sessions plays a prominent role in many corporate cultures, where there is a deeper history of group problem solving and the need for quick generation of ideas. Brainstorming techniques can be used to access the best thinking about a marketing concept or to develop new products and services.

Historically, schools have focused much less on group work and creating a "product" and more on the long-term goals of individual learning, growth, and achievement. Additionally, schools have not granted high status to novel concepts, unique applications, or challenges to the knowledge presented. Student work is often evaluated in highly constrained formats based on the retention and synthesis of information provided by text and teacher. Now, both school and business cultures are beginning to reward those who think independently, work in teams, cogenerate new ways of doing work, and, to a

certain degree, challenge the system of pre-
scribed knowledge and acceptable truths.

Since the late 1970s, a range of brainstorming techniques called webbing, clustering,
semantic mapping, mindscaping, and mindmapping have become more popular in many
schools. Most of these processes have similar
techniques, each generating from a central
point on a page to the outward perimeters to
fully capture a concept, much like a spider
spinning a web to trap flies. Most of these techniques inspire a unique blend of intellectual
curiosity and artistic expression that contrib-
utes to the construction of knowledge, as presented most vividly in the recent applications
of brainstorming webs for educators by Nancy
Margolies (1991).

The first systematic use of webbing in
schools was to facilitate students' fluency of
ideas during prewriting activities. The process
of writing has always depended on the generation and recombination of ideas, but the "process writing" approaches developed in recent
years have highlighted the need for students to
generate and connect a large quantity of ideas
before sitting down to a first draft. After the
first draft is complete and the refining and editing steps begin, the brainstorm web is often left
behind, a mere relic of the creative beginning of
the paper.

But brainstorming webs now are used
across disciplines for more than seeking out the
initial kernel of an idea. They are used to develop students' fluency with thinking. Fluency
with linear and nonlinear thinking is a critical
dimension of learning, as critical as fluency

with reading and writing, which are both primarily linear forms. Fluency is the capacity to
flow flexibly from idea to idea within and
across disciplines, easily make interconnections
among ideas, sustain inquiry over time, openly
pursue alternative points of view, question and
possibly discard hardened opinions, and get "un-
blocked" when faced with a difficult task.

By gaining visual fluency, students become
aware of their own generative thinking patterns,
the unspoken linkages between thoughts and
feelings, and the more subtle metaphorical understandings derived from connecting and bridging
usually unconnected ideas in a holistic meeting
of one mind, or many. The byproduct for teachers is that they gain precious, authentic insights
into the interior designs of students' thinking.

Many of the initial brainstorming techniques used in schools were based on the trans-
lation of early brain research showing that the
mind does not process information solely in list-
like, linear patterns. Tony Buzan, developer of
the "mindmapping" process, grounded his work
in the brain specialization research conducted
by Roger Sperry, Robert Ornstein, and others.
Summarizing this research, Buzan states:

> In most people the left side of the
> brain deals with logic, language, rea-
> soning, number, linearity, and analy-
> sis; ...the right side of the brain deals
> with rhythm, music, images and imagi-
> nation, colour, parallel processing, day-
> dreaming, face recognition, and pattern
> or map recognition (1979, p. 14).

A foundation to brainstorming webs is that
the integrated facilitation of the "whole brain"

is essential to the learning process. A second foundation is the visual dimension. We all daydream and make free associations on a moment-to-moment basis—in our minds. It is a part of the human condition. Yet, when these associations become more focused by the individual and are put into visual form, there is an added capacity for seeing the holism of the ideas, making more associations, reorganizing concepts and details *as images*, and then communicating these *ideas as images* to others. This is when brainstorming in the mind moves outward to others and becomes a useful tool for collaborative work.

One of the most prevalent misconceptions about using brainstorming webs is that they are a simple, one-step process of visually linking free associations without special technique. Some educators may even associate brainstorming with a lack of intellectual rigor. Practiced with depth, brainstorming webs offer students the opportunity to break the stiff intellectual molds of the "behavioralist" classroom and to spin new interpretations and construct new forms of knowledge.

Importantly, brainstorming webs are usually guided by focus questions or a defined objective, such as "What is my topic?" or "What do I need to produce?" Several webbing techniques promote the retention of details and lead to the further organization and analysis of ideas. Brainstorming webs are not just starting points but can evolve in sophistication in relationship to any task. If there is a "mistake" in the use of these visual tools it is that we ask students to stop the webbing process too soon and immedi-

ately move on to revision and structuring of a product instead of motivating students to deepen and strengthen the conceptual linkages of their first vision.

Uses of Brainstorming Webs

While brainstorming webs are the most idiosyncratic of visual tools—empowering students to generate the form of the graphics and associations themselves—there are well-developed techniques and guides for linking isolated ideas and enhancing patterns. Gabriele Lusser Rico, an early developer of webbing techniques, brings an artistic sensitivity to the process of writing by directly linking the development of clustering and webbing techniques to seeing patterns, seeking personal understanding, and envisioning metaphors. In *Writing the Natural Way*, Rico leads writers through a transformative process based on visual brainstorming:

> In the beginning you will relearn the fresh, childlike attitude of wonder through clustering; later you will develop your inborn receptivity to pattern making through the trial web,… reclaim the ability to think metaphorically, reconcile opposites to build creative tension, and balance original vision with revision (1983, p. 20).

The clustering technique begins with very little graphic guidance or rule governance. A word is written in the center of a page, surrounded by an oval, and then associations are extended by using lines and curves to other ideas. This type of "trial web" is a short step

FIGURE 3.1

A Trial Brainstorming Web

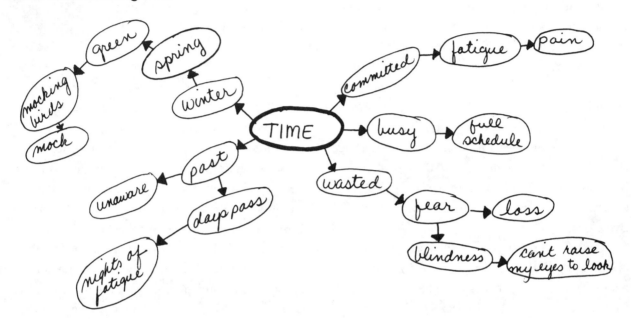

Source: Rico, G.L. (1983). Writing the Natural Way. Los Angeles: J.P. Tarcher, Inc. Reproduced by permission.

beyond the unstructured brainstorming clustering: Central ideas are identified, expanded, and linked together (Figure 3.1). Rico thus makes only a slight distinction between the initial brainstorm called a *cluster* and the conscious structuring of ideas into a revised form called a *web*. The use of these open-ended techniques for prewriting and revision are focused on developing students' fluency with the generation of ideas and not for highly developed organization. After this prewriting stage, students are instructed in writing a rough draft using the linked information.

While Rico and other proponents of process writing approaches have developed and clarified

the use of clustering for different forms of writing, Tony Buzan developed more specific "mindmapping" techniques for adults and younger learners for the purposes of generating ideas, taking notes, developing concepts, and improving memory (Buzan 1979). Joyce Wycoff has written a book called *Mindmapping* (1991) for personal and business applications, based on Buzan's work. Her mindmap for defining mindmapping (Figure 3.2) reveals that this approach may involve a range of different images and self-created organizational structures and types of uses.

Buzan's approach, similar to Rico's, begins with a key word or image in the center of the page, followed by extensions radiating outward

FIGURE 3.2

A Brainstorming Web: Mindmapping

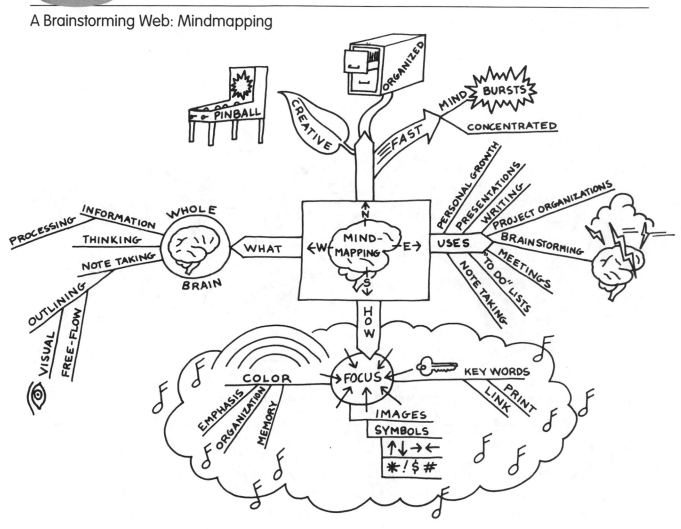

Source: Wycoff, J. (1991). Mindmapping. New York: Berkley Book. Reproduced by permission.

(Figure 3.3). Buzan is much more specific than Rico about the actual drawing and lettering of mindmaps. Notice that the linkages in this mindmap on economics are shown extended from the key idea in the center; secondary ideas are connected to each other by arrows and lines in other areas of the map, with more important ideas drawn nearer the center. Additionally, all words are printed in capitals, and single words are suggested for each line.

Buzan also makes suggestions for creating advanced mindmaps that are more "holographic"

A Student Example of Mindmapping

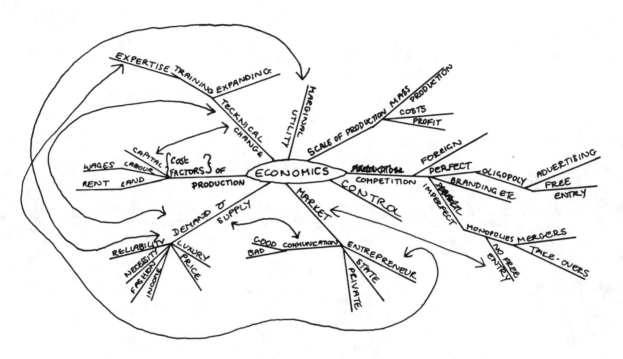

Source: Buzan, T. (1979). <u>Use Both Sides of Your Brain.</u> New York: E.P. Dutton. Reproduced by permission.

in appearance. Graphics are enriched by adding highlights such as arrows, symbols such as asterisks and question marks, geometric shapes, three-dimensional drawings, and unique images. Multiple colors are also key to making each mindmap a mnemonic tool. All of these techniques are intended to make recall easier for the individual and information more accessible to others, much like a cartographer would design a map for easy use by readers.

Though Rico suggests a second-level trial web and Buzan provides a few advanced map-ping techniques, both approaches promote sustaining students' abilities to create idiosyncratic, integrated, holistic views of connected information across disciplines. This really means that techniques and uses of brainstorming webs should not be overly defined.

Because of the open-ended nature of brainstorming webs, these types of visual tools have been used by curriculum developers for breaking through hardened discipline boundaries to create and investigate interdisciplinary units of study for students. Heidi Hayes Jacobs (1989), a leader in interdisciplinary design, has created a four-step Interdisciplinary Concept Model that uses a brainstorming "wheel" for constructing units (Figure 3.4). The finalized version of this elementary level unit design on the topic "Flight" was generated through a process of:

1. Identifying the organizing center
2. Brainstorming associations related to the organizing center using the disciplines
3. Devising a set of essential questions to frame the unit as a scope and sequence
4. Generating activities and assessments under each essential question for implementation.

This brainstorming "wheel" seems much more structured than the webs in Figures 3.1–3.3; the planning wheel is a finalized document that evolved from various drafts leading from an initial organizing center.

What is most effective about the use of the brainstorming wheel is that students and teachers have a common tool for becoming co-curriculum designers. Jacobs believes that there are three basic "design sources" for building an interdisciplinary unit, each reflective of students' levels of familiarity with the organizing center of the unit of study: If students are unfamiliar with the topic or theme, then teachers are the primary source; if students have some basic knowledge of the topic, the wheel may be used together by students and teachers; and, if the topic or theme is student-centered, the design source may be the students (Jacobs, personal communication, March 3, 1996). This direct linkage of teachers and students to the construction of curriculum—*with a visual tool as the concrete medium for communication*—may become an essential element of the co-construction of knowledge in classrooms.

Jacobs believes that a key to the development of any of the initial designs generated by students or teachers is to go beyond the brainstorming web or wheel to a more structured and detailed graphic for building the unit of study. We must not leave students with a partial view of a design process in which they become partners, but help them to further scaffold and construct interdisciplinary connections. How? One way to enrich the brainstorming wheel is through continuing to focus on the questions that "frame" the organizing center. In this way, the wheel is turned, revised, and focused until more key concepts surface that will support long-term learning. Looking ahead to the next three chapters, another way to deepen the design process is to apply a task-specific organizer, a thinking-process map, and multiple Thinking Maps to the initial wheel of information. These other visual tools may provide pathways for the fourth step in this design: generating activities and assessments related to the framing questions.

Mindmapping and clustering are really the historical forerunners for the development of other dynamic visual tools. Webs are uniquely suited for developing creative forces of mind, but as shown in the previous samples, the ideas generated from a first cluster or mindmap also may lead to revision and to forming greater organizational structures and deeper analysis. Brainstorming webs are used to promote linkages between and among ideas in mostly non-

FIGURE 3.4

Flight Planning Wheel

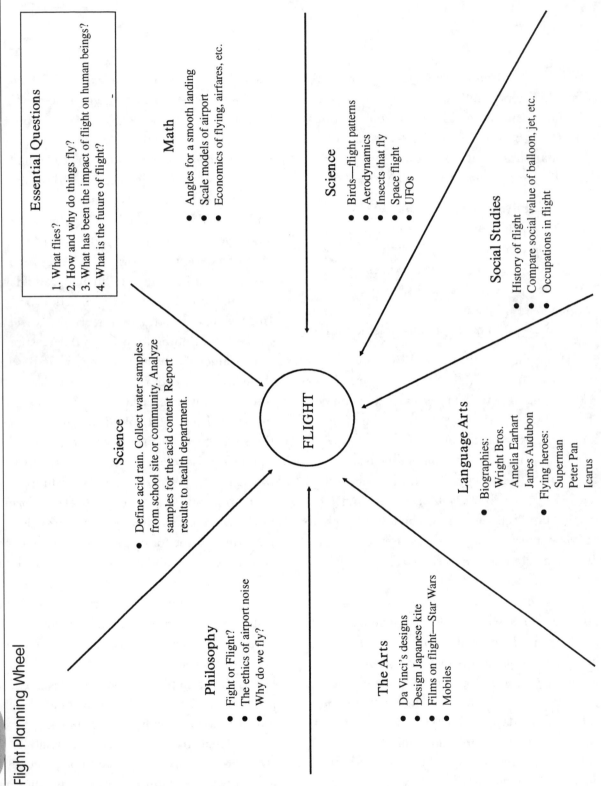

Essential Questions

1. What flies?
2. How and why do things fly?
3. What has been the impact of flight on human beings?
4. What is the future of flight?

Math

- Angles for a smooth landing
- Scale models of airport
- Economics of flying, airfares, etc.

Science

- Birds—flight patterns
- Aerodynamics
- Insects that fly
- Space flight
- UFOs

Social Studies

- History of flight
- Compare social value of balloon, jet, etc.
- Occupations in flight

Science

- Define acid rain. Collect water samples from school site or community. Analyze samples for the acid content. Report results to health department.

FLIGHT

Philosophy

- Fight or Flight?
- The ethics of airport noise
- Why do we fly?

The Arts

- Da Vinci's designs
- Design Japanese kite
- Films on flight—Star Wars
- Mobiles

Language Arts

- Biographies:
  Wright Bros.
  Amelia Earhart
  James Audubon
- Flying heroes:
  Superman
  Peter Pan
  Icarus

Source: Jacobs, H.H., ed. (1989). Interdisciplinary Curriculum: Design and Implementation. Alexandria, Va.: Association for Supervision and Curriculum Development.

linear patterns and tend to inspire personal connections, experiences, and creativity as foundations for learning.

Brainstorming Webs for Individualized, Cooperative, and Schoolwide Learning

Webs are relatively formless beginning points that evolve and generate from the patterns and graphic representations of the thinker. As we will investigate in the following two chapters, this design decision is unlike task-specific graphic organizers and thinking-process maps, which are much more structured upon introduction. Webbing involves more and varied techniques rather than any predetermined form. This difference is important as we think about how to use webs to support individual, cooperative, and schoolwide learning—and later as we think about which type of visual tool is most useful for different work. As you read these sections and the following chapters, keep in mind that brainstorming webs are not necessarily used before organizers or thinking-process maps. Any of these tools may be used at any point within the teaching-learning-assessing spiral.

Individualized Learning

Brainstorming webs are highly integrated, holistic, seemingly without a point of completion, usually unstructured, and idiosyncratic. As an individual student uses webbing over time, what evolves is a personal, visual language—or

secret code—with its own graphic forms, drawings, linking arrows, color scheme, and individualized iconography. Thus, brainstorming webs should be honored as "sacred" in the sense that the free associations and links among ideas are more like an evolving piece of art than a document to be evaluated using comparative methods. Within this framework of respect for individual thinking, there is no "wrong" use of webbing, only more productive techniques that students can learn for improving their abilities to tap the flow of their creative juices.

An individual's abilities for generating, remembering, and organizing ideas are improved through webbing. Extensive brain research, starting with George Miller's "magic 7" in the 1950s, has shown that the more students are able to "chunk" information, the greater the chance for retention of this information. One common example of chunking is the conscious design of U.S. telephone numbers into a primary chunk of seven numbers, with an added chunk of three for the area code (555-555-5555). Often, students do not link information, and the result is that they have an unpunctuated string of phrases and sentences that are not held together in an organizational pattern.

A concrete example is found in the daily requirement for note *taking*. Even the word *taking* implies merely passive consumption. A particularly effective and reflective use of webs is for note *making*. Instead of writing down the linear strings of words spoken by teachers or found in texts, students actively "chunk" or draw conceptual linkages among the bits of information being delivered. When students are asked to study for a test, retention is often improved because they have acted on and remade the information, stamped it with their own design. When a written paper is assigned using this information in webbed form, students create notes that have been personalized instead of offering tired prose based on repetition or plagiarism of a teacher or text. This is really one of the secret successes of all visual tools: Students must take an active role in the formation and reformation of knowledge.

From a teacher's point of view, brainstorming webs also are useful as a platform from which a student may more easily verbalize ideas. Students often feel on the spot, insecure, and an easy target for criticism when asked to speak, especially about a complex concept (many of which are nonlinear). Some of this insecurity is because of time constraints. There may not be enough wait time (Rowe 1974) for students to think about and then verbalize a complete response to a question. Teachers who ask students to "think aloud" (Whimbey 1995) their ideas from a brainstorm web will bring even more understandings than by reviewing the web alone, because the web itself is not a complete expression of ideas and connections.

On a deeper level, because of the lack of knowledge or the inability to explain all of the nonlinear connections among ideas, a student may mentally stutter and fumble. Webbing provides built-in wait time, a safety net, and a new way to find out what and how a student is thinking. The insight gained from listening to a student while looking at his or her web is inspiring because it provides an additional representation

system for seeing into the unfettered, generative mind of the individual. By verbally articulating the relationships established by visual means, students improve their abilities to understand and seek patterns and interrelationships, the foundations for concepts.

Cooperative Learning

The value of brainstorming webs is enriched many times over when they also are used for cooperative learning and group problem finding and solving. This is because the generative process of one mind when linked with others produces a platform that reveals commonalities, new ideas, different perspectives, and alternative solutions that will lead to new learning. This cooperative work also expands and stretches into a new shape each individual's web of knowledge. There are three common ways of using brainstorming webs in cooperative groups and classrooms:

- sharing webs already created by individuals,
- creating a brainstorming web in small groups, and
- facilitating whole-class webs.

In the first case, students are given a topic and then asked to brainstorm webs on their own. Individuals are then organized into groups to share their visual representations. When students work in a group to share their already generated brainstorming webs, the wide array of graphic depictions is exciting, mentally exhausting, and sometimes confusing.

It may not be productive to have each group member present or explain his or her idiosyncratic graphics and complex associations; rather, students can use the webs as notes from which they may add ideas to the group discussion. Group members also could pass each paper around the table to look at individual webs. From this scanning routine, major ideas and details are usually identified and organized into a group web. Students who are not as verbal or active in cooperative groups often come alive when they have a brainstorming web to speak from. These same students also are supported as they try to clarify their ideas, because they may use their web as a guide to their thinking.

Another option is for all group members to generate a single brainstorming web without individuals first creating their own graphic display. This may be accomplished by having a single page in the center of the group for all to add to as they discuss a topic. Alternatively, the group may have a facilitator develop a brainstorming web with their input. The facilitator can use a paper in the center of the table, a chalk or white board, or a computer with software such as Inspiration (discussed later in this chapter).

The facilitator "draws out" ideas from the group and creates a web. It is important to realize, though, that because of the idiosyncratic process of brainstorming webs, the further the creative process goes from individual control of the web's development, the greater the need for talented facilitators to collect and link ideas. Thus, in group brainstorming, the facilitator must continually check with the individuals to ensure that their ideas are being fairly represented on the web.

This concern about facilitation is even more important when brainstorming webs are used by teachers in front of a whole class. During this process, the group has ceded control of the graphic design and structure to the teacher. This is far from a trivial move. If a facilitator, teacher, or student controls the form of the ideas, consciously—and often unconsciously—he also guides the construction and ultimate form of knowledge for the group. Thus, brainstorming webs always should be understood as changeable and negotiable. *If the teacher is more interested in "correcting" or editing ideas to fit a lesson, the whole purpose and process of brainstorming webs has been lost.* A student in the class should be able to safely say, "This is not how I see this connection!" which could be the literal truth.

The visual dialogue that ensues during and after constructing views of knowledge is the key to group brainstorming. Teachers and students may later step back from the fully developed web and begin to reorganize, delete, and redraft the picture of knowledge. But this is a significant next step away from brainstorming and may necessitate the use of other strategies and possibly another type of visual tool.

Schoolwide Learning

When brainstorming webs are used schoolwide from year to year, it establishes a constantly renewing focus on personalized learning and creativity. If a whole faculty decides to reinforce the use of brainstorming webs, key intellectual dispositions are facilitated: individual creativity; fluency with ideas; enjoyable and collaborative problem solving; the active integration of knowledge; and respect for different perspectives, learning styles, and intellectual frames of mind.

This kind of commitment by a faculty requires initial training on brainstorming techniques and follow-up. This training includes webbing for note making and writing processes, structures for individual and cooperative learning using webs, reading across the disciplines using webs, and suggestions about how teachers can lead students to different levels of webbing and into how to integrate webs with other strategies and visual tools and to a final product. Unfortunately, most faculties may receive, at most, only a two-hour workshop on brainstorming, and this will usually concern a discrete application such as prewriting. This beneficial but surface level understanding of the power of webbing is only a starting point for developing the skillful use of this type of visual tool by teachers and students alike.

Obviously, the reinforcement of brainstorming webs honors creativity of mind. Webs that include many colors, multidimensional drawings, icons, and a wide array of graphic symbols provide a link between the world of artistic expression and academic work. This fluency with ideas needs year-to-year reinforcement for development. It is crucial to the facilitation of creativity that brainstorming webs are student-centered tools used over multiple years.

Each of the traditional areas of creative study has tools: the painter with brushes and canvas, the musician with an instrument, the sculptor with hands and carving knives, the woodworker with finely crafted saws and chis-

els. We thrive as human beings when we use tools, the extension of our multiple intelligences. What does the creative thinker have? Brainstorming webs. When brainstorming webs become an integrated part of learning in a school, the hallways become filled with this intellectual artwork, side by side with students' murals and posters.

In a schoolwide approach, the unique and highly personalized perspective of the individual is honored from year to year as students reveal their open-ended perceptions of knowledge, from personal and cultural knowledge to conceptual understandings of content. How one "sees" the world is represented in the personalized, graphic language of webbing. When this personalized language is reinforced throughout a school, individual students have a safe intellectual haven for investigating their own thinking and a creative tool for life's long journey of learning. The individual is further honored when his or her ideas are continuously integrated into webs created in group problem-solving sessions and classroom discussions. There is no better approach for building self-worth than by asking a student to show what *and* how she is thinking (whether by visual tools or other means); self-worth is heightened when this personalized view of knowing is added to a group product.

Linked to the idea of honoring individual creation of ideas over time are the significantly different forms of the ideas that students communicate by using webs. The ideas are holistic and integrated, rather than isolated answers to specific questions. Unencumbered by linear, formal usage that both speaking and writing require, the dynamic, nonlinear form of webbing elicits interdependencies rather than isolation of facts. As students become comfortable with these tools over several years through a school-wide effort, they are naturally inclined to expand their horizons and seek interdisciplinary connections within and among concepts rather than within the boundaries of specific content areas.

Software for Brainstorming Webs

The most productive technologies for brainstorming webs generally are not found on software but with paper and pencil, chalk and chalkboard, or multicolored dry-erase pens and a large white board. Those teachers and students who have been using brainstorming webbing of any kind may reject, out of hand, software-based brainstorming technologies. Hold on to this skepticism, because for some people brainstorming necessitates the physical link of a mind-to-hand sketched web on a large piece of paper, created with highly idiosyncratic sketches, drawings, and doodles. However, don't let your doubts prevent you and your students from working on the computer with highly generative graphics programs that are created explicitly for brainstorming.

One of the essential elements of brainstorming is the capacity to make nearly unconscious connections and associations between ideas, letting the mind spill onto the page without interference or filters of any kind. Of course, most graphics or "draw" software programs give users the capacity to create the graphics for brainstorming webs, such as ovals, boxes, and lines. With most programs, however, this is extremely

time-consuming and counterproductive for the techniques of brainstorming webs.

Brainstorming is linked to the intuitive quickness of mind and should not be filtered through cumbersome technology. Any brainstorming tools need to at least come close to the capacity of the hand to quickly link graphics and write phrases in the graphic. At this point, few software programs meet this need.

One of the most advanced software programs being used in industry and, more recently, schools is called Inspiration (for information about this and other software programs, see "Selected Resources for Visual Tools" at the end of this book). Inspiration is partially based on the pioneering work of Gabriele Lusser Rico and Tony Buzan, and it reflects many of the qualities of webs discussed previously. As shown in this prototype example by student Brian Cooper (Figure 3.5), the software provides the capacity to generate multiple graphics across multiple-linked pages, pull-down word processing windows, basic icons for pasting into clusters, and multidirectional arrows and curved lines.

As with most dynamic software programs, Inspiration has more capacity than you see here. Two important features set Inspiration apart from other software programs of this type. First, students from mid-elementary grades and up are able to rapidly create and link graphics with the touch of a key. Second, the graphics and the text are linked so that the graphic automatically expands as more text is typed. This is an essential requirement of high-quality software for any kind of dynamic visual tool. If students cannot quickly add text within a graphic without

FIGURE 3.5

A Prototype Student Web Using "Inspiration" Software

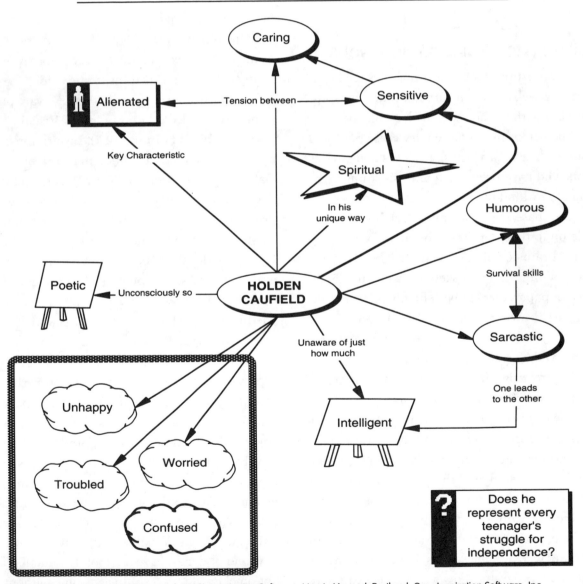

Source: Helfgott, D., M. Helfgott, and B. Hoof. (1992). Inspiration Software, User's Manual. Portland, Ore.: Inspiration Software, Inc.

having to reshape it, the thinking is interrupted by laborious attention to creating the graphic rather than generating and connecting ideas.

Inspiration also includes basic flowcharting capacity, a draw palette, and organization hierarchy formats that are used much like thinking-process maps. The information that students generate using these hierarchy formats is directly linked to the traditional outline form so that both forms are available at the touch of a button. Students can then proceed to writing using a pull-down word processing window.

These capacities provide the near ideal application of brainstorming webs in the computer environment. Given the constraints, of course, this and other software programs only approximate the ideal of brainstorming. Yet Inspiration also gives students and teachers benefits that hand-drawn webs don't provide. First, the webs are much neater and thus more readable by others. Second, webs are easily saved in memory for immediate recall and as continuing documentation of students' growth. Finally, the capability to continually rework and revise a web is possible without having to recopy the entire graphic. This benefit is analogous to the time before word processors when it was necessary to painstakingly rewrite drafts by hand or typewriter; now we save the original draft on computer and try out alternative patterns of ideas. With software such as Inspiration—and other programs we discuss in the chapters ahead—revising ideas is quick and fun and motivates students to try out different configurations of thoughts and thus deepen thinking.

Some students may have success starting with brainstorming on the computer, but the idiosyncratic nature of brainstorming calls for starting students with an array of colored writing instruments (crayons, pencils, pens, chalk) and a writing surface. Students should really have the experience of developing their own private language and visual code before being constrained by the graphics offered in the computer environment. After students have developed their own visual style, highly flexible and quick software is a next tool that they can control and mold to their own mindfulness.

Brainstorming Webs and Assessment

As discussed previously, brainstorming webs may be highly idiosyncratic in form and open-ended in function. Given these qualities of webs, teachers need to accept a student's web as an often incomplete, *evolving* construction. The web is an offering for serious conversation and as a platform for moving toward differently organized, finalized work. Because of the lack of common rules, visual graphics, and icons, webbing and clustering are best suited as beginning and midrange tools for learning. They are not reliable as a basis for formal, teacher-based assessment. Tony Buzan's more systematic techniques for mindmapping make clarity of communication easier and thus make some form of assessment possible; brainstorming webs, however, are usually used for generating, organizing, and assessing, and not for end-product evaluation.

As the next two chapters show, task-specific organizers and thinking-process maps hold much more promise as assessment instruments because students often use a common and flexible graphic form.

These cautionary notes should not prevent webs from being used *informally* for pre- and post-assessment purposes. They also can be collected over time in students' folders and portfolios. A wide range of webs created by a student over multiple years may help demonstrate the student's improving abilities to create and communicate patterns of ideas. Reviewing students' webs also shows growth in the areas of specificity of language use, deletion and reorganization of ideas, and the ability to synthesize information into concepts. Brainstorm webbing may also be attached to a final draft of a product—such as a piece of writing, oral report in social studies, or a science project—as a way for students to document their work. As shown in Figure 3.4, a brainstorming web may show quite succinctly how a student sees the interrelationships among key concepts and details within an entire subject area. This demonstration of knowledge, though not formalized in a traditional format, provides an authentic representation of students' understandings.

Ironically, brainstorming webs do offer one of the richest ways for a teacher to gain a wealth of insights into a student's thinking and learning, because of the very fact that students are expressing their ideas without fear of failure or concern about being assessed. One-to-one interviews or conferences with students using their web to explain their ideas provides teachers with a holistic view of how students connect ideas. Having students verbalize their visual presentation increases the chance that they will be more open and communicate the fullness of their ideas, because all of the scaffolding for the ideas are readily available and may be shown to the teacher. The teacher's task when viewing

and listening to the student is to remain open and nonjudgmental, ask coaching questions that stimulate further thinking and reflection, and engage the student in a conversation of depth and meaning.

The greatest value of webbing for assessment purposes may be found in the area of student self-assessment and the development of metacognitive behaviors. With a web, a student has the opportunity to see his or her own thinking develop through this visual lens. Just as an architect may step back from a blueprint and imagine the building that will be constructed from this design—and thus assess this important document—so too the student creating a web leans back and literally re-*views* the big picture context of interconnected ideas and the detail work that will lead to a final product.

This metacognitive dimension of brainstorming webs is probably the most essential quality of these tools: Individual students are able to look upon their own thinking and the personal connections they have made without external evaluation. It is their safe mental space to see the holism of their ideas, and to think about, deepen, and improve their own styles of thinking. It is a pool of their own thinking. Yet, students also must be able to step back from this reflecting pool and look at other patterns of thinking. As we move on to investigate another type of visual tool, we will see that the power of creating personal, visual patterns also may be enhanced by using common organizational patterns that have evolved within certain content areas and for particular tasks.

Task-Specific Organizers

I f teachers from across the range of teaching styles can agree on one thing, it is that lack of organizational abilities is the ultimate academic downfall of many students. Teachers' desperation echoes in the hallways of elementary schools and colleges alike: "If only my students could organize their ideas!"

This need for organization is a major reason why task-specific organizers—often called "graphic organizers"—are spreading rapidly through schools at every grade level and across all disciplines. In addition, technology is driving the need for organization skills. Students in cyberspace are finding too much unrefined, unorganized, irrelevant information.

In terms of Benjamin Bloom's Taxonomy of Educational Objectives (Bloom 1956) the intellectual capacities to analyze and synthesize information (organize, break down, and reformulate) are the steps upward toward evaluative thinking. Yet, even the lowest level of Bloom's taxonomy—knowledge—is defined as the basic *organization* of content. It is no wonder, then, that most students have difficulty at complex tasks. They have the intellectual capacity, but do not have the intellectual tools for constructing, patterning, and reforming information into meaningful, organized knowledge. Most students—especially in the bottom tracks in our educational system—are stuck responding to low-level "comprehension" tasks above which they may never have a chance to rise. We can change this pattern by using visual tools.

Importantly, *even the most basic level of organization of information is inherently conceptual*. Unfortunately, retention of isolated content knowledge by rote memorization is overly emphasized instead of retention through the development of organizational designs and conceptual understandings. The general processes of organizing information require that learners go well beyond the retention of isolated bits of information. Students must have the know-how to analytically *construct* interrelationships so they can *evaluate* knowledge. This process takes mental energy, perseverance, and much more. It also can take the support of focused linear and nonlinear organizational tools that reflect different content-specific patterns of knowledge and conceptual structures.

Task-specific, or graphic, organizers are visual tools for managing and displaying information. The term *task-specific* is used here because most of these visual tools are created specifically for learning a skill, following a process for a defined task, or organizing information within a content area in a pattern that is highly specific to that particular body of knowledge. These organizers also are used for more global tasks, such as guiding students through a complex set of connections in an interdisciplinary unit of study.

Some of these organizers border on being static displays of information. These include charts, matrices, and axis diagrams, all of which are used mostly for charting preformed information for presentation and further analysis. These are graphic displays that teachers and researchers have used for generations, but most of these visuals are not "tool like" and thus not a pressing concern of this book.

Examples of task-specific organizers range from story maps for reading comprehension to decision trees in mathematics to flowchart languages for computer programming. Unlike brainstorming webs, these graphics are usually highly formalized, teacher created, refined, and rule governed to fit a specific content learning process. Students are taught a certain visual design and systematic process for using the graphics and text to guide them through a task. Flexible use is sometimes encouraged but only within the boundary of the task.

Although brainstorming webs and task-specific organizers may seem worlds apart, both draw on the ever-present power of visual representations to show interrelationships, though in a different way and with a different purpose. Webbing primarily facilitates the unbridled generation of ideas with idiosyncratic graphics and secondarily promotes organizational structure. Whereas creativity may be a by-product of some graphic organizers, each task design is primarily a supportive guide for organizing ideas toward a specific outcome. Though all visual tools may be used concurrently, task-specific organizers often are used as beginning and midrange tools on the way to creating a final product, much like using two outline organizers as research is being conducted and before the actual writing of a research paper.

Outlining: The Unbearable Task

When most educators think of organizing information, a certain (horrible) process comes to mind: the oft-dreaded outline. In tandem with 3×5 cards, the outline has been the most powerful way to harness immense amounts of information for research and writing. Outlining may remain the ultimate intellectual bootcamp for students heading off to advanced training in higher education. Yet, every year teachers see that though a few students actually enjoy using this form, many more create outlines after they have completed a paper—and only then because it was required to complete the assignment. Many teachers confess that they did the same when they were in high school.

Students entering the work force need the organizational ability embedded in the outline, but most are frustrated with the formulaic process. Teachers are equally frustrated by the sometimes torturous process of teaching the intricate numbering, lettering, and indentation system.

The central point here is that nothing is sacred or irreplaceable about the actual formula and format for traditional outlining. What *is* irreplaceable is the essential need for organizing information. Although the outline may be useful and worth learning, the same kind of multilayered task has shown to be more easily accomplished—and with the same level of quality—using several visual tools.

For example, the cognitive complexity of the outline is daunting to students. They are required to create a hierarchical category structure of ideas:

I.
  A.
    1.
      a.
  B.
    1.
      a.
  C.

Simultaneously, they must show the sequential pattern in which information will be delivered by paragraphs or chapters (I, II, III, IV).

This parallel processing is too heavy a cognitive load for most students. Alternatively, a process using two separate task-specific organizers simplifies and clarifies the work by visually identifying the two steps toward completion. A simple example of this may be seen by reviewing the two figures in the Introduction of this book (Figures I.1 and I.2).

First, a hierarchical tree structure is used to collect, analyze, and finalize a main idea or theme of a paper in relationship to supporting details. Once the conceptual work of showing interrelationships is completed, a flowchart is used to generate the sequence for the inherently linear presentation of those hierarchical relationships in writing. The student may then use the traditional outline form, or most likely go directly to writing a first draft of the paper with a big-picture view of the processes. Such use of these two organizers does not necessarily replace the traditional outline, but it makes the mental *out-lines* of the task visible, understandable, effective, and, not incidentally, enjoyable to construct.

Uses of Task-Specific Organizers

As we will see in the pages ahead, the addition of a range of task-specific organizers to the classroom repertoire provides students with a variety of patterns for organizing information. Many task-specific organizers are designed by curriculum writers and published within texts for use by students, or they are created by teachers as they become fluent with developing organizers that fit their needs.

Resources are available—books full of graphic organizers developed for specific tasks—and some of the examples in this section draw from these works. The purpose of many of these organizers may be first for the teacher to present and model the use of the graphic, using content information, and then later to coach students to use the organizer as a flexible tool to complete a similar task within the same content area. But this is not always the case.

There is a growing tendency toward inflexible modeling and static use of task-specific organizers. This usage may be both a blessing and a curse. It can be a blessing because students are, at a minimum, learning about useful organizational structures. This is definitely a step up the cognitive ladder, but it does not necessarily lead to students' actively constructing knowledge using these tools. The curse is that some graphic organizers are now being made avail-

able to teachers and students in prepackaged pads of organizers or blackline masters with few instructions. They are distributed to students and then used repetitively as glorified fill-in-the-blank sheets. The interactive, constructive, and reflective capacities of these tools are lost in this low-level mode of delivery.

As the next section shows, these same task-specific organizers may be used in dynamic ways for reading comprehension and learning across content areas.

Reading Comprehension Across Disciplines

Research in the area of reading comprehension has been a training ground for the cross-content development of task-specific organizers to guide students in analyzing basic text structures in various types of reading. Reading teachers and researchers know that as students gain a basic fluency with language and expand their vocabulary base, they also build a storehouse of linear and nonlinear schemata reflecting the pattern of relationships found within written selections.

Task-specific organizers are used to mirror these linear and nonlinear text models as closely as possible. Based on specific text patterns, these organizers are guiding tools for students as they read and translate linear text into differently organized patterns. The flip side of these applications is that the organizers also become assessment tools when teachers see how students demonstrate their organization of the themes and conceptual relationships found in texts.

These organizers are taught to students as tools for constructing, comprehending, summa-

FIGURE 4.1

Human Interaction Outline

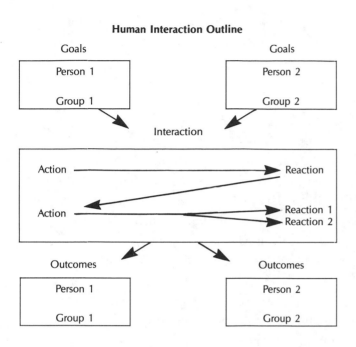

Human Interaction Outline

Source: Jones, B.F., J. Pierce, and B. Hunter. (December 1988/January 1989). "Teaching Students to Construct Graphic Representations." Educational Leadership 46, 4: 20–25.

rizing, deleting, and synthesizing ideas found in the text. Jones et al. (1988/1989) present nine different generic organizers for comprehending text, including the Human Interaction Outline in Figure 4.1. This flexible organizer is used for investigating any kind of human interaction, but it is often used specifically as a guide for reading in history.

The authors identify several "key frame questions" related to the graphic. Using the relationship between European settlers and Native Americans, a teacher may ask: Who are the persons or groups? What were their goals? Did they conflict or cooperate? What was the outcome for each person or group?

It is important to notice that these are typical teacher questions. But the organizer provides the concrete tool for teachers and students to further organize, analyze, and synthesize information that stretches across dozens of pages, throughout a whole book, or from several sources, including computer databases. The authors describe the implications for students when they use this application and other text-structure based organizers for reading comprehension:

> Reading with an appropriate graphic structure in mind can help students select important ideas and details as well as detect missing information and unexplained relations. Moreover, constructing and analyzing a graphic helps students become actively involved in processing a text. Graphics foster nonlinear thinking, unlike prose summaries and linear outlines (Jones et al. 1988/1989, p. 21).

It is essential to recognize the term "constructing," because the authors are elevating the graphic beyond the work of organizing basic information and toward the outcome of creating meaning from text. Multiple research findings in the area of text-structure organizers led the International Reading Association to state that this approach embodies a significant new set of tools used "between reader and text by which meaning is found and created" (International Reading Association 1988). It cannot be overstated: After students become experienced in using these tools flexibly and in response to the text structure, they actively construct and demonstrate their view of *meaningful relationships.*

Text structure as a basis for improving reading comprehension also has been linked directly to writing process instruction by showing that organizers enhance students' abilities to read and then to summarize, in writing, what they have read (Armbruster, Anderson, and Ostertag 1989). Using control groups, Armbruster's research showed that students who learned the common text structure of "problem-solution" (Figure 4.2) in the social studies area at the 5th grade level created summaries that were rated significantly higher on the quality of their writing, which included organization, focus, and integration of information (see Armbruster et al. 1987).

The problem-solution tool shown in Figure 4.2 is amazingly simple and scaffolds students' successes—two reasons why visual tools are successful, especially for low-performing students. This simplicity is only a starting point for flexibly applying the form to more complex structures and interrelationships. This organizer is introduced to students, and then the actual creation and expansion of the graphics is led by individual students (or cooperative groups) in response to the complexity of texts. Unfortu-

nately, many preset organizers fall prey to becoming static outlines for students to fill in.

Content-Specific Applications

In social sciences research, the fundamentals of reading and writing take on great importance. Students read page after page and chapter after chapter of detailed information on different cultures, seek to understand conflicts in history, and to reconcile their own life with the past. Many of the task-specific organizers for reading comprehension and writing are used in social studies to show the interrelationships of details to main topics and causal relationships, which often form the basis for historical analysis.

An example of a task-specific organizer is called backmapping (Figure 4.3). In this example, the class was given a research question about Vermont state geography, which asked for causal relationships among geological and geographic history and present culture. The question itself seems overwhelming, but a 6th grade teacher worked with students to guide them to an understanding of these relationships that span the millennia. By using these organizers, students acted on and re-formed the ideas bound in the linear text. Students were able to organize information, see different points of view, and thus begin to make more reasoned judgments and evaluations based on the factual record. These organizers provide the structural foundation in analysis and synthesis for evaluating knowledge.

Although brainstorming webs have been used in schools almost exclusively in the areas of reading and writing, task-specific organizers

FIGURE 4.2

Problem-Solution Text Structure: Frame and Definition

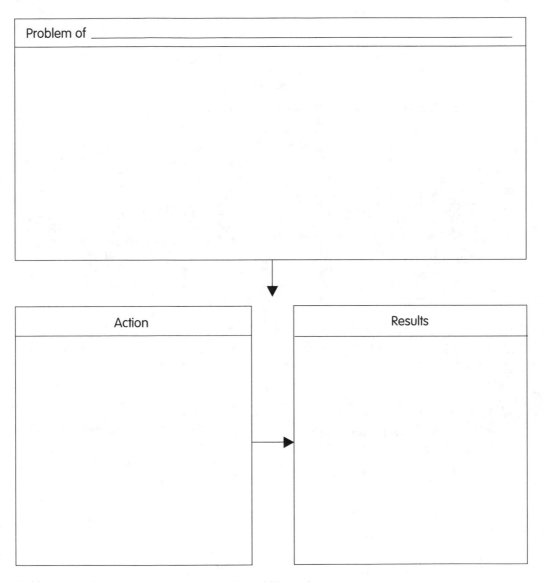

Problem = something bad; a situation that people would like to change
Action = what people do to try to solve the problem
Results = what happens as a result of the action; the effect or outcome of trying to solve the problem

Source: Armbruster, B.B., T.H. Anderson, and J. Ostertag. (November 1989). "Teaching Text Structure to Improve Reading and Writing." The Reading Teacher 43, 2: 130–137. Reproduced by permission.

FIGURE 4.3

Backmapping Task-Specific Organizer

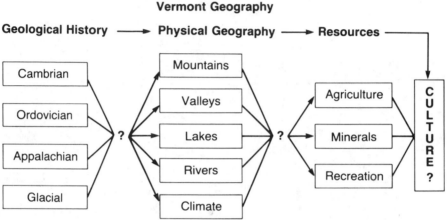

Question: How does the geological impact of the last three periods affect the physical geography that now plays a part in our culture?

Vermont Geography

Geological History → **Physical Geography** → **Resources**

Cambrian, Ordovician, Appalachian, Glacial ? Mountains, Valleys, Lakes, Rivers, Climate ? Agriculture, Minerals, Recreation → CULTURE ?

Source: Clarke, J.H. (1991). Patterns of Thinking. Needham Heights, Mass.: Allyn and Bacon. Reproduced by permission.

actually had their beginnings in mathematics, science, and, most recently, computer science. In mathematics instruction, pictorial representations and graphic symbols have been used to represent and work through problems. The National Council of Teachers of Mathematics (1990) strongly endorses the use of mathematical modeling using different graphics for solving problems and for making connections to other disciplines. The standards presented by this council state that:

> Students who are able to apply and translate among different representations of the same problem situation or of the same mathematical concept will have at once a powerful, flexible set of tools for solving problems and a deeper appreciation of the consistency and beauty of mathematics (National Council of Teachers of Mathematics 1990, p. 146).

Flowcharting for solving word problems, the use of sorting trees for grouping activities, and Venn diagrams are three traditional organizers that have provided the foundation for simple to complex mathematical thinking.

The example in Figure 4.4 is taken from a lower elementary lesson in the "Math...A Way of Thinking" program (Baratta-Lorton 1977). First, the teacher models how to develop the tree to group information, using the categories "big" and "little." The class then proceeds

FIGURE 4.4

Sorting Tree

Teacher: [Working on a transparency in an overhead projector, using a pile of assorted buttons and a marker] This is called a sorting tree. I'll demonstrate how to use it. I put all my buttons next to this top line and write "button." What is a way we divided the buttons into two groups before?

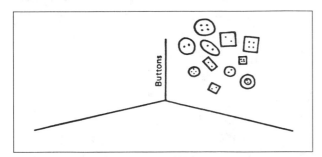

Student: Big and little.

Teacher: Okay. I'll divide the buttons into big and little and move the two new piles to the two places where I have written "big" and "little" on the sorting tree.

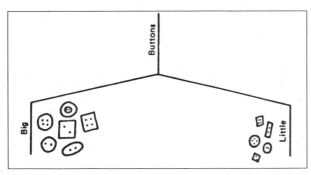

What is another way we divided the buttons?

Student: Round and straight.

Teacher: I'll write "round" and "straight" on these branches of the sorting tree and then move the buttons to the correct branches.

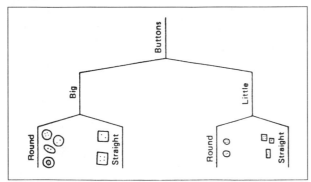

Another way?

Student: Two holes and four holes.

Teacher: Okay. I'll write that on the branches first, and sort the buttons by two holes and four holes.

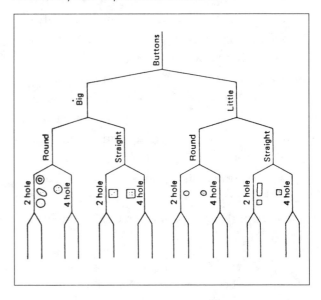

Are there any other ways we sorted the buttons?

The process continues until the students run out of ideas for dividing the buttons, there is no more than one button on each end branch, or there is no more room on the tree. Then, they divide piles of buttons on their own copies of the sorting tree. Students who wish to, may work together and record their joint efforts on a single sorting tree. Any words they need spelled are written in their spelling notebooks.

The assignment is to divide the buttons into continually smaller groups until no more space remains on the tree or there is no more than one button on each end branch. Each new division is recorded on the appropriate branches.

As the students work, the teacher asks the following questions: Does sorting the objects in a different order make any difference? Would the smallest piles on the overhead have turned out differently if we had sorted the buttons by two holes and four holes first, then by round and straight, and last by big and little? If it makes a difference, why? If it doesn't, why not?

Source: Baratta-Lorton, R. (1977). Mathematics...A Way of Thinking. Menlo Park, Calif.: Addison-Wesley. Reproduced by permission.

through several sorting steps to a completed tree. But this is not the end. The next standard question from a constructivist teacher is: Are there any other ways we sorted the buttons? Students are then asked to review the visual representation of buttons and begin to create a new tree, possibly starting with categories based on color, number of holes, or shape. Of course, this activity is first conducted with manipulatives, but over time, students must make the transition from using concrete manipulatives to more abstract concepts that do not translate easily into touchable entities. The visual depiction of concepts thus provides the bridge from concrete manipulates to abstract, visual representations.

In mathematics, the Venn diagram may be the most widely recognized visual tool for representing category membership and general-specific relationships. The Venn diagram is now used across many disciplines for categorization as well as for comparing similar and different qualities of things. Wandersee relates the history of the Venn diagram:

> Venn (1894) pointed out that logicians borrowed the use of diagrams from mathematics during a time when there was no clear boundary line between the two fields. Line segments, triangles, circles, ellipses, and rectangles were all used to diagram categorical propositions during the early development of logic as a discipline (Wandersee 1990, p. 927).

With this background information, Wandersee has developed concept circle diagrams based on the Venn diagram for science education (Figure 4.5). The concept circles look similar to Venn diagrams, but they are not used in the same way. The concept circles are modified to highlight additional information about concepts and not strict category relationships. The category is named in the center of each circle. The overlapping circles of different sizes and colors (up to five circles in any one cluster of circles) may represent the concept both quantitatively or qualitatively. The use of "telescoping" circles, as represented by dotted lines, links, and circles, shows related concepts, progressive differentiation, and subordination.

This wide range of applications for task-specific organizers in various content areas confirms that visual representations are not confined to any one discipline. In fact, it is this tremendous versatility of visual tools that makes this area so exciting and ripe for interdisciplinary applications (Clarke 1991). The proven effectiveness of these tools for supporting students' comprehension of information and conceptual understandings also reveals that these are not merely mechanical structures for rote learning. Another dimension becomes apparent by reviewing these different applications: A few simple graphics such as lines, boxes, and arrows provide the conceptual linkage among bits of content information to form complex, meaningful, holistic images that students can easily grasp and mentally manipulate.

Using Task-Specific Organizers for Individualized, Cooperative, and Schoolwide Learning

As shown in the previous discussion, task-specific organizers provide teachers and students with isolated structures for content

FIGURE 4.5

Concept Circle Diagrams for Science

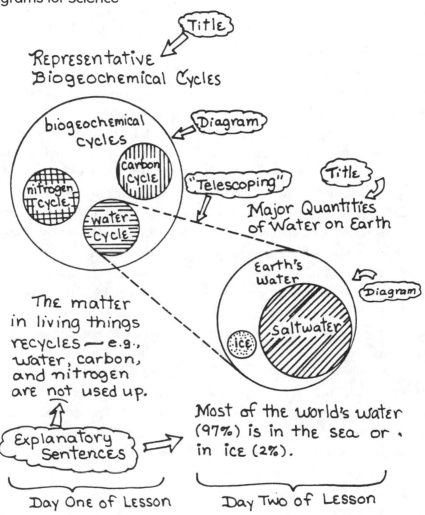

Source: Wandersee, J.H. (1990). "Concept Mapping and the Cartography of Cognition." Journal of Research in Science Teaching 27, 10: 923–936. Reproduced by permission.

learning and for developing content-specific skills. These specialized visual tools are useful for individual, cooperative, and schoolwide learning. As you read ahead, consider how these tools—as common starting points—provide a schematic foundation from which all students in an inclusive, heterogeneous classroom can succeed and expand their vocabulary, basic skills, and conceptual understandings of content knowledge.

Individualized Learning

No matter how well a lesson plan is articulated and delivered by a teacher, students often moan, "But *what* do I *do*?" In most lessons or units, students have a clearly defined end-product, such as a written document, oral presentation, written book report with drawings, choreographed skit, diorama, or written responses to a set of questions. The bridge between the assignment of work and the end product—what students actually are going to do—is often the vital, missing link in classrooms. This is because the process of giving students the minute details for solving every task takes away the joy of learning, creates a dependent learner, reduces the chance that students will practice solving problems using their own learning styles, and, in practical terms, is not possible because of time constraints. Thus, we may all know the silent answer to the question of what to do: "I'm not going to tell you. You need to figure that out for yourself!" The implication is that the students have—or should have—the organizational capacities to complete the task. Individual learners *do* have this capacity; they just may not have the tools for *activating* this capacity.

Organizers provide one answer to this problem. These visual tools can do double duty by helping the teacher clarify a stated set of objectives and giving individual students—especially students with special needs—a tool to complete the task.

An organizer such as the problem-solution in Figure 4.2 provides a guide for interpreting a reading selection with this specific kind of text structure. A teacher may first use this organizer as a medium for conveying a holistic view of the process of the task. An organizer also conveys the complexity of the task as broken down into visual stages (problem definition, action, re-

sults) and the expectations for finally leading to the intended outcome of the lesson. Individual students may then take this organizer as an effective tool for working through the comprehension problem on their own. They are not given the answer, but a concrete outline and tool for constructing the answer. Of course, the organizer needs to be developmentally appropriate and have been modeled and practiced in the classroom so that individuals will know that the tool can be changed and redesigned to fit the particular selection. If this modeling has not occurred, then individual students may end up filling in the blank boxes of the organizer.

Teachers and teacher assistants may then use the organizer to mediate the learning process of individuals in one-on-one settings. Individual students' concepts and misconceptions are revealed by simple graphic guidelines for showing interrelated knowledge. The detailed structure of these visual tools supports individual students who are having a difficult time with a particular task, such as steps in solving an algebraic equation or outlining a research paper. A more highly specified, preformed organizer may be created by the teacher, according to special needs of students (high, average, or low performing), to provide guidance, feedback, and greater chance for success in the future with complex tasks. This chance is greater because the student has been given practice with the organizational pattern required in the middle range of problem solving.

As with any tool, the task-specific organizer has inherent constraints. Because the organizer is usually teacher produced, focused on isolated tasks, and not easily transferred outside of the task, students may remain dependent on the teacher for guidance for when and how to use the organizer. To improve students' flexibility and use of these tools, different types of organizers need to be thoroughly introduced, not as teacher assignments but as student tools that can be redesigned. Students should be encouraged to create their own task-specific organizers in response to a task at hand. A long-term outcome would be that individual students would have a small collection of organizers that they use regularly, each crafted by teachers or students for applying essential skills and understanding key concepts reflective of the patterns and processes of each content area.

Cooperative Learning

The back-and-forth rhythm that is created in a cooperative learning classroom between the individual and the cooperative group is greatly enhanced when organizers are brought into the picture. Whereas brainstorming webs are idiosyncratic and sometimes inefficient for sharing knowledge, task-specific organizers are usually well defined by the task, graphically consistent, and easily exchanged among students with varying levels of performance.

Using a decision tree in mathematics, a computer flowchart, or a story map in cooperative groups is highly effective for supporting the linkage between individual to group work. This happens by assigning one or several task-specific organizers to individuals for completion before meeting in cooperative groups. Individuals then come to the group with a visual presentation of their ideas within a common structure used by

other participants. This information design motivates the efficient communication of ideas and provides practical tools for establishing individual accountability that many teachers require for group work.

The Think-Pair-Share format (McTighe and Lyman 1988) is a strong instructional design for building this linkage. Next, using the problem-solution reading text structure as an example, individual students may first read a selection that evolves into a classic problem-solution text structure. The individual students first structure and generate their analysis using the problem-solution organizers, creating the pattern on their own page, and thus showing their view of the problem-solution. Then students shift into pairs and create a new pattern, a synthesis of their two organizers. Finally, two or three pairs move into a cooperative group setting (with appropriate group rules) and construct a final version of the organizer depicting their group view of the problem-solution. Each group in the classroom may then present its final organizer to the whole class.

As with individualized use, task-specific organizers give added focus to a group because of the efficiency, effectiveness, and accountability grounded in the graphic. Having used a common visual tool, all participants in the classroom are able to easily read the graphic and make comparisons among different constructions when group leaders then present their cumulative problem-solution organizer.

This kind of sequence facilitates key capacities in students: generating individual patterns of ideas, sharing these ideas in groups, seeking and analyzing patterns of ideas, redrafting ideas through incorporation, synthesizing different perspectives, and evaluating completed ideas. These "conceptual" and "product" outcomes, moreover, are complemented by outcomes with much deeper implications—interpersonal outcomes. Interpersonal outcomes are crucial to cooperative learning: The students in pairs and cooperative groups are engaged in verbal *and* visual discussion, negotiation of meanings, and dialogue. And all students in the group are guided to show the full pattern of reasoning behind their answers so that the dominant voices in groups are supported in patiently *seeing* other perspectives. The entry of a visual tool into discussions thus elevates the communication to a new level: We must construct, listen, and see if we are to understand.

Schoolwide Learning

Use of these tools schoolwide is successful through consistent and developmentally appropriate use. When students enter a school where organizers are used across grade levels and subject areas, a problem is quickly apparent—a problem for students. Consider what would happen over time, grade to grade, as each year a student is introduced to a completely new design for an organizer by a new teacher for the same content task! Effective use of task-specific organizers by students over multiple years within a whole learning community (school or district) depends on consistency of design and repetitive use of the tool; if not, confusion triumphs over clarity.

In a whole school, teachers collaborating within a content area or across grade levels

need to work together and decide which organizers are the most valuable for their students. The criteria include clarity of design, consistency in use, flexibility, and developmental appropriateness (see Chapter 6, "Thinking Maps," for suggested criteria and characteristics). The tool should be flexible enough to be structured differently depending on the developmental level so that students become highly proficient in its use as more advanced work is required from year to year.

For example, if teachers in an elementary school or English teachers at the secondary level agreed that they would all use the Armbruster et al. problem-solution text structure with students, students year after year would become highly proficient with and develop automaticity in analyzing text selections using this format. The degree of sophistication in use of the tool would vary from grade to grade, but the basic format would remain relatively constant. Another example might be a series of task-specific organizers for "the scientific process" in which each major stage of the process from problem finding to evaluation of a hypothesis could be represented as an organizer. This kind of linking of multiple task-specific organizers is powerful within a single classroom and has profound implications if used from one grade level to the next within a school, or vertically within a school district.

Of course, both teachers and students have a major concern: too many task-specific organizers. After several years of elementary school and many secondary classes, a student could be inundated with literally hundreds of task-specific organizers directly reflecting content-driven procedures, skills, and strategies. These organizers show up in textbooks, on software, and in the work of teachers and students. Though each of these graphics may provide a clear structure for approaching each task, taken together they may be overwhelming. Some new resource books have an endless supply of "graphic organizers" related to specific topics, duplicated and ready for students to use. Unfortunately, this process moves away from the quality of "tool-like" use that is promoted in this book.

If a school faculty decides that these kinds of visual tools are useful for schoolwide use, it is strongly recommended that teachers agree to use only a handful of highly effective task-specific organizers in each content area that will work best for students as they proceed through the grade levels.

Software for Task-Specific Organizers

Much like the graphics that are now commonplace within a lesson or unit of study in textbooks, task-specific organizers are for the most part found as graphics within extensive software programs based on content learning. Many educational software programs are filled with static graphic organizers, most often as simple flowcharts for guiding students through procedures and not as visual tools. Like the Inspiration brainstorming software discussed in the previous chapter, many general use and educational software programs have "draw" capabilities that permit students to create organizers.

Because of the content-related foundation of task-specific organizers, few stand-alone programs exist for these types of visual tools. One software program that uses these organizers as the centerpiece of instruction is called MacMapper. It is used to systematically link reading comprehension across disciplines and writing process using organizers. Students are taught a range of different, relatively static graphic patterns primarily related to text structures and discourse forms. Each tool is also defined by an underlying thinking process.

This program, developed by Richard Sinatra (St. Johns University) was originally based on three simple generic semantic maps (Figure 4.6) (see also Cronin, Meadows, and Sinatra 1990). These tools, formed of arrows and different-sized rectangles, developed into three configurations: sequencing events for plot analysis, identifying themes, and classifying information. Students are given reading selections that are structured to specifically highlight these patterns so that they can seek them out when reading.

The most recent version of MacMapper has incorporated several more organizers based on the task of comparing characters and narrative organizational structures. Sinatra reports that this software helps students move from highly structured forms to constructive learning:

> Using these highly structured computer programs, students learned to construct visual maps representing the relationships of major ideas, subordinate ideas, and explicit information (Sinatra 1994).

FIGURE 4.6

Generic Semantic Maps

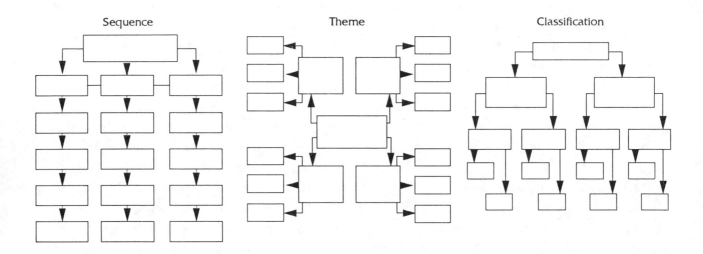

Source: Cronin, H., D. Meadows, and R. Sinatra. (September 1990). "Integrating Computers, Reading, and Writing Across the Curriculum." Educational Leadership 48, 1: 57–62.

Notice that the underlying processes of sequencing and classification are graphically represented for showing plot and main idea, respectively. This software and materials package is thus situated in the gray area between task-specific organizers and thinking process maps, and this may be why the approach has had success. Results of reading and writing tests of students using Mac-Mapper software and the accompanying workbooks show that this kind of explicit patterning of information related to content specific needs—with little possible variance by students in the beginning—can directly change student performance on tasks such as identifying the plot and main idea of the story. Sinatra (1994) and collaborating researchers found that, in general, research points to an obvious need of low-performing readers for effective instruction in both reading and writing:

[Readers] who are weak in sensing the organizing structure of stories and who lack the strategies for uncovering story relationships have difficulty with recall and comprehension....[And] writers who are taught to organize ideas in writing so that the reader will readily uncover the organizational structure will be better communicators and, therefore, better writers (Sinatra 1994).

This direct linkage among reading, writing, and computing is made explicit by task-specific organizers that guide students to discover and then use the basic organizing structures found in texts. Using this software, students are engaged, as well, in constructing their own organizers for writing reports.

The only visible drawback to this program is the high degree of visual similarity between the design components of each organizer (only rectangles and arrows). Each of the organizers has a different configuration, but is composed of boxes. Though this obviously has not prevented successes, independent communication between students and teachers in a classroom and a whole school may be impeded because of the lack of unique graphics related to specific tasks. Fortunately, this software program also has a "draw" capacity, much like other drawing programs, so that students and teachers may develop their own configurations and variations.

This software is not simply something to load onto the machines in a computer lab. Teachers involved in this approach receive in-depth training and modeling on how to use the organizers in the reading and writing process in the computer environment *and* in day-to-day teaching in the classroom. This kind of training in computer use sets the right direction for linking work in the classroom to computer laboratories. Ultimately, all teachers will need to be computer literate. Possibly, the use of visual tools for organizing ideas and information will be a concrete bridge linking daily classroom instruction, based on facilitating organizing abilities, and the computer structures graphically and flexibly used by students.

Task-Specific Organizers for Assessment

Task-specific organizers are on nearly the opposite end of the assessment spectrum from brainstorming webs. Because organizers are usually based on teacher-directed processes, outcomes, and content-driven expectations, organizers may provide a clear picture of student comprehension of information and concepts. In fact, task-specific organizers are particularly well suited for pre- and post-measures of student learning; thus, we are seeing these forms show up on standardized tests.

For example, when a student is given a flow-chart organizer for showing the steps in the scientific process and then afterward is asked to use this tool for working through another similar investigation, the teacher gains one picture of the growth in the student's knowledge. If this flowchart is then actively used to organize data during the application of the scientific process, the teacher has an additional, comparative measure of comprehension and application of a process as it relates to learning a concept. These pre- and post-instructional techniques also may be included as artifacts in a portfolio, showing how a student at a certain point during the year was understanding and applying the scientific process.

Though task-specific organizers may be useful for student interviews and helpful for students to self-assess their learning of specific tasks, the highly structured form of many organizers seems to fit the pre-post assessment format. These preformed organizers are now showing up on statewide tests because educators and test-makers are becoming more interested in *how* students are working through problems as well their "correct" answers. Many testing instruments, using both closed and open-ended formats, require that students show their work. This requirement is most evident on statewide, holistically scored writing tests. Students are given space and guidance for prewriting on the test format and then asked to turn in these notes with their final draft. Task-specific organizers designed to reflect certain types of writing prompts—such as narrative, comparison, and persuasion—are effective tools for demonstrating how the student generated and organized ideas as a first step toward responding to the prompt.

Standardized tests also are beginning to include organizers as an integrated part of the exercise format. In an example from a North Carolina State Reading Test (Figure 4.7), students read a story and then have two organizers for the task of identifying character traits. These organizers give a cluster of character traits for two characters in the story, Ooka and the shopkeeper, with a general term (*stingy*) that summarizes in one word the main character trait of the shopkeeper. The array of information for Ooka is missing only the summary term (*fair*).

Though this "organizer completion" format does show whether a student can chose a correct summary term given an array of organized information, it falls well short of the possible uses of task-specific organizers for assessment. Of course, this format is part of a standardized,

multiple-choice test, and the test makers provided too much information and limited the development of the graphic. This graphic is not being used in a tool-like way and thus is not a valid instrument for assessing a student's capacity to further comprehend a reading selection.

An alternative use of this organizer format would have given students a partially completed pair of diagrams for both characters with additional information provided below. Students would have had to correctly show which trait fit the appropriate character in addition to identifying the summary trait for Ooka. An even more authentic use of the character map would have been for students to create their own map of the information, but obvious practical problems exist: Students across a state or throughout the United States are not using a commonly defined organizer for this task.

A second example, this taken from a new standardized nationwide English Language Arts Assessment instrument (CTB/McGraw-Hill 1996), is a more open format (Figure 4.8). This text design guides students from reading comprehension to a writing prompt using the "character" organizer as the medium. After reading a three-page story, students complete the graphic. A scoring rubric ("0" to "3") is used, with the high score of "3" given to full and appropriate completion of the graphic. This task-specific organizer is then used by students as a prewriting tool for responding to a writing prompt. Students' writing is then scored on the basis of logical structuring of ideas and mechanics. This example shows more productive use of a visual tool than the previous text sample, but remains

FIGURE 4.7

North Carolina State Reading Test: Character Diagram

1. Which word best completes this diagram or character map?

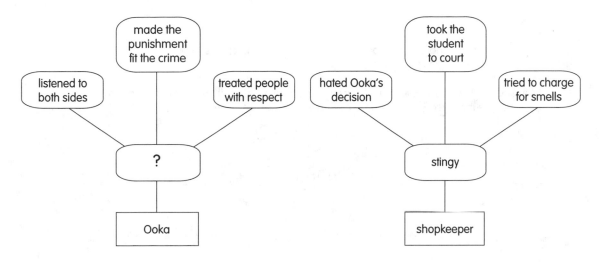

A honest

B fair

C tricky

D miserly

Source: North Carolina State Department of Education. Reproduced by permission.

a static framework that is filled in by students, rather than being expandable to show greater depth of thinking.

That task-specific organizers are showing up on standardized tests is an indicator that these and other kinds of visual tools are gaining popularity across the United States. The promise of visual tools for integrating teaching, learning, and assessing in classrooms and across larger learning communities is growing. This point of integration will become even more apparent as we investigate a third type of visual tool: thinking-process maps. The next two chapters show how visual tools based on fundamental thinking processes offer a way for students to construct and investigate patterns of thinking, as well as provide students and teachers with a common framework and language for transferring fundamental thinking patterns across disciplines.

*

FIGURE 4.8

English Language Arts Assessment: Reading and Writing

1 Choose one character in the story who is interesting to you.

• Write the name of that character in the circle.

• What does the character say or do that tells you what kind of person he or she is? Write one example in <u>each</u> large box.

• What do these actions tell you about the person? In <u>each</u> small box, write one word to describe the person, based on the actions you chose for the large boxes.

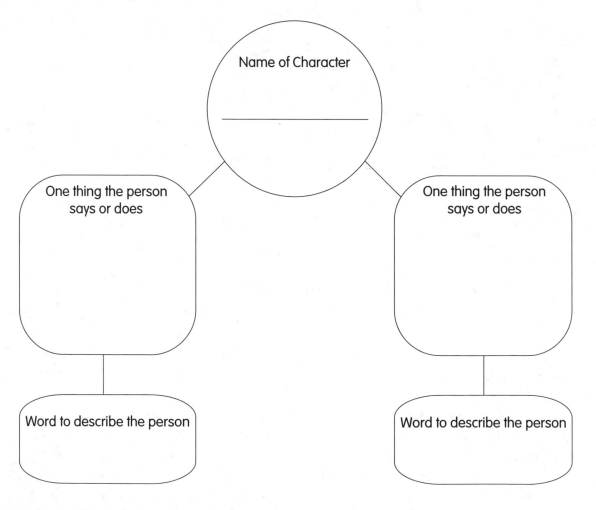

Source: CTB/McGraw-Hill. (1996). <u>English Language Arts Assessment.</u> New York: Author. Reproduced by permission.

Thinking-Process Maps

I've seen a "Hagar the Horrible" cartoon that reflects the Information Age in three words. Hagar is standing with his hands on his hips, exasperated, yelling at a small creature: "I'm going to say this once, and only once: THINK! THINK! TIIINK!" That humor hits the mark for parents, teachers, and employers as we remember ourselves saying the same thing, wanting our children to think through life's problems in the home, classroom, community, and workplace.

The Information Age has pulled many of us from our past moorings, turning employment in manufacturing jobs into "higher-order" positions requiring the capacity to design robotics that, in turn, replace even more manufacturing jobs. High-paying jobs require the abilities to create, organize, design, implement, and evaluate—in short, to think. This technological age also brings us closer to each other—by airplane, phone, or computer network—requiring each of us to work closely with others worldwide who hold different perspectives that often reflect different ways of knowing. A central demand of all these changes is that we need to find new ways to collaborate, communicate our thinking, and negotiate meanings.

Thinking-process maps are visual tools defined by fundamental and more global thinking processes, from constructing simple categories to developing new theories. Unlike task-specific organizers or brainstorming webs, thinking-process maps are visually designed to reflect fundamental patterns of thinking. Before looking closely at these tools, let's investigate how they evolved to become student-centered tools for transferring thinking processes across disciplines.

The Transfer of Common Thinking Processes

Unless severely brain damaged, we human beings are all born with a common brain-based array of fundamental thinking processes and the unique capacity to use sophisticated tools to extend these processes. Despite the endless nature-nurture debate, I.Q. testing controversies, and "Bell Curve" theories, few would deny that our brains and sensory capacities enable us to sequence events, identify attributes, classify information, make predictions using cause-effect reasoning, make decisions by comparing alternatives, reason analogically, and identify part-whole relationships.

The term *capacity* is important. As we mature, we each have the possibility for continuous growth in our capacities to use these processes. Consider if parents and teachers actually had to start from scratch—from a cognitive tabula rasa—and train students how to use these cognitive processes. Impossible. Such training would be analogous to torturous attempts to write artificial intelligence programs for a computer so it could perform even the simplest tasks. So when a teacher exclaims "Think!" she is asking students to draw from these deeply held powers of cognition. Of course, for this rallying cry to be authentic, the teacher *must believe* in the efficacy of each student's capacity for intellectual growth.

Balanced with social and physical development, a child's intellectual development has been at the heart of the educational mission for public schools for all children in society since their inception early in this century. As discussed in the first chapter, this mission has been heightened in the Information Age with the development of constructivism as a guiding philosophy for education in the United States and other countries. The rise of the so-called "thinking skills movement" of the past 20 years has been driven by extensive cognitive science and brain research showing that we, as educators, can facilitate and improve students' intellectual abilities. Benjamin Bloom's (1956) *Taxonomy of Educational Objectives in the Cognitive Domain* has been a key element in this shift. Teachers have been trained and retrained to ask facilitating questions that require students to analyze, synthesize, and evaluate knowledge.

Many instructional approaches introduce strategies to students so that they have ways to respond to higher-order questions. A wide array of theoretical and practical programs—upwards of 50—is available for the teaching of, for, and about thinking (Costa 1991). The range of these programs is truly amazing: from simple cognitive skills activities in workbooks to creativity programs such as deBono's (1970) Lateral Thinking, to in-depth mediation of thinking with Feuerstein's Instrumental Enrichment, to Richard Paul's critical thinking "Socratic" approach, to Matthew Lipman's (1985, 1991) Philosophy for Children program. The critical response to these programs is also wide, as some thinking skills programs—although called "thought provoking"—have been disparaged as mere add-on materials for already overburdened teachers.

The difference between an add-on thinking skills program and one that creates long-term effects may be found in the degree to which these processes transfer into different content areas. One of the essential, unanswered questions that goes to the center of the cognitive revolution is this: Do thinking processes transfer across content areas? David Perkins, one of the recognized leaders in the field, cowrote an article with Gabriele Soloman in 1989 about this question. Importantly, Perkins and Soloman suggest two types of transfer: low road and high road.

Low-road transfer is attained through a developed automaticity in the use of a cognitive process, such as classification, by way of repetitive use of the skill in a variety of content learning contexts. High-road transfer is attained when the student is able to consciously transfer a learned, abstract principle from one situation to another. Here is their summary:

> Thinking at its most effective depends on specific, context-bound skills and units of knowledge that have little application to other domains. To the

extent that transfer does take place, it is highly specific and must be cued, primed, and guided; it seldom occurs spontaneously (Perkins and Soloman 1989, pp. 16–25).

Allowing that transfer does occur, but in most cases with some content-specific knowledge needed, Perkins and Soloman argue against the strict dichotomy often made between teaching process skills and isolated content knowledge:

> The heart of the synthesis we would like to suggest challenges this dichotomy. There are general cognitive skills; but they always function in contextualized ways, along the lines articulated in considering the philosopher's habit of mind (Perkins and Soloman 1989).

These capacities for low- and high-road transfer of processes and principles into different contexts is crucial for understanding the complexity of thinking-process instruction and the power of thinking-process maps as visual tools for transfer, whether high or low.

Webs, Organizers, and Thinking-Process Maps

It is clear that brainstorming webs are highly idiosyncratic and used primarily to facilitate associative, creative processes. Less clear is the distinction between organizers and thinking-process maps. We have seen that task-specific organizers are created in response to a specific content task. But each of these organizers, viewed from the perspective of thinking-process instruction, is also based on fundamental patterns of thinking. Usually an organizer is implicitly grounded on one or several fundamental thinking processes, but explicitly guided by a teacher's content-driven outcome. The following review of thinking-process maps shows that they are theory-embedded tools for transferring thinking processes into different content contexts.

Thinking-process maps are similar in appearance to task-specific organizers, but with an additional important outcome. Each is *introduced* to students as a fundamental thinking pattern and used for direct improvement in their thinking, metacognitive abilities, and reflectiveness—as well as content learning. The intended purpose is twofold. Students will improve their understandings of specific content skills (low-road transfer) and content concepts (high-road transfer). In addition, these thinking-process maps will support the improvement of students' thinking abilities over time.

In summary, the basic and sometimes fuzzy distinction between task-specific organizers and thinking-process maps is this: Organizers are visual tools that teachers often present to students to complete a context-specific task, whereas thinking-process maps are visual tools that teachers introduce to students ahead of time so they can create *their own transfer* of thinking processes to content-specific tasks.

Uses of Thinking-Process Maps

One of the early approaches to using thinking-process maps for improving general prob-

lem-solving and thinking abilities was Albert Upton's (1940/1961) work at Whittier College in California starting in the late 1950s. In *Creative Analysis* (Upton, Samson, and Farmer 1961), a text created from Upton's years of experience in teaching his introductory semantics course, students were introduced to a view that language was guided by fundamental thinking processes. Upton also employed a few basic diagrams for explicitly teaching students how the fundamental *creative and analytical* processes used by scientists (taxonomy, anatomy, and physiology) are similar to the thinking processes that we use to communicate with each other every day.

The traditional classification diagram was one of these tools for developing formal, hierarchical relationships, such as for establishing types of printed characters (Figure 5.1). Because Upton was interested in meaning-making in general, he taught students to use this diagram to transfer this thinking process across disciplines: for creating taxonomies in the biological sciences; or for showing less formal category structures, such as identifying the theme, supporting ideas, and details in a novel; or in social studies for organizing research information.

Upton also showed students that this highly analytical classification tree was key to creating and ordering one's own view of knowledge:

> It is quite possible that your classification (diagram) differs from ours in the number of levels, in the number of sorts, and/or in the terms themselves. A classification is "right" to the degree

FIGURE 5.1

Creative Analysis Classification Tree

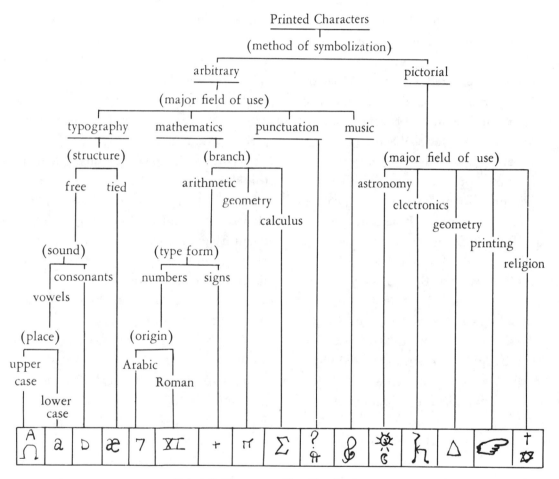

Printed Characters Classification #2

Source: Upton, A., R. Samson, and A.D. Farmer. (1961). Creative Analysis. New York: E.P. Dutton. Reproduced by permission.

that it names qualities relevant to purpose and names enough qualities to fulfill that purpose.... Do not waste time designing a neat diagram. Use plenty of paper so that your diagram may grow. The neatness may come later if you wish, but the fundamental purpose is to order your thoughts so that you can make up your mind (Upton et al. 1961).

After 35 years, these words about the rightness, relevance, and supporting evidence of answers still stand strong as a constructivist's description of knowing. A fundamental thinking process is defined, activated by a visual tool for showing relationships, and ultimately driven by the purpose of "making up your mind" and acting.

As Hechinger reported on the front page of the *New York Times* in June 1960, the Upton approach significantly changed his college students' scores on the Bellevue-Wechsler intelligence test. These changes came about through in-depth applications of cognitive processes and accompanying "diagrams" in problem-solving groups. This approach became the foundation for a comprehensive language arts program called THINK! which was implemented in schools during the 1970s and early 1980s and later brought about significant changes in Scholastic Assessment Test (SAT) scores (Worsham and Austin 1983). These first uses of thinking-process maps in the THINK! program were the experiential, practical, and theoretical forerunners of the Thinking Maps approach (see the next chapter).

Much like Upton's early work, a range of thinking-process maps is currently used for improving students' thinking processes. Before looking at samples, consider the purpose for thinking-process maps. As mentioned previously, many graphic organizers (task-specific organizers) now available provide little or no guidance in how to use thinking-process maps for constructive thinking. The same graphic design may be used for several distinctly different thinking processes and may be introduced to students through highly inflexible, fill-in worksheets.

If we want students to flexibly transfer thinking processes within and across disciplines, we need to encourage clarity of definitions for these processes, some consistency in form related to each, and the dynamic use of these visual tools. Otherwise, in the long run, students will become dependent on the worksheet, confused and bored by just another graphic organizer.

Positive examples abound showing how thinking-process maps may be introduced to students. Most of these maps are explicitly designed to facilitate the most commonly used cognitive processes, such as sequencing (flowcharts), cause-effect reasoning (fishbone diagrams), classification (tree diagrams or Venn diagrams), and comparisons (a variation on the Venn diagram).

In *Organizing Thinking*, Sandra Parks and Howard Black (1992) offer an array of different thinking-process maps, including interval graphs for ordering and sequencing, central idea graphs, class relationship diagrams, and a compare and contrast diagram. Each of these tools is presented to students as grounded in a thinking process; then, sample content transfer applications are offered for practice.

For example, teachers are given an introductory blackline master for the compare-or-contrast diagram (Figure 5.2) and then provided with practice lessons for using the document to compare concepts across different disciplines. Students use the tool to compare concepts such

FIGURE 5.2

Compare/Contrast Thinking-Process Map

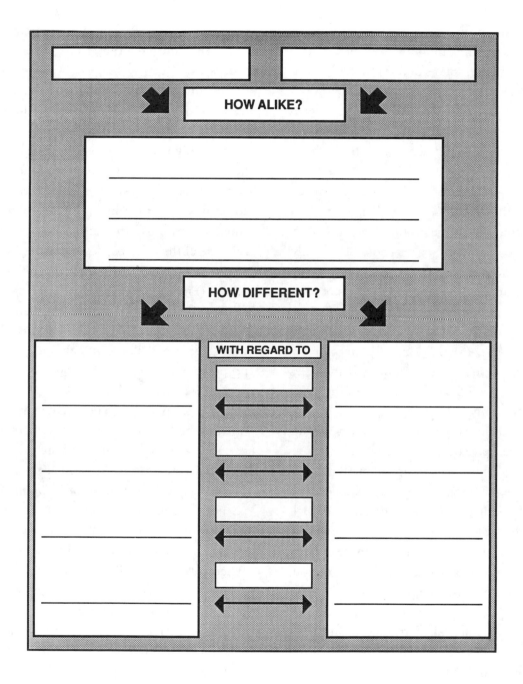

as nouns and pronouns, state and federal government, the Plains Indian Family and today's family, and amphibians and reptiles.

Parks and Black (1992) are showing students, in visually detailed steps, the fundamental processes of comparing. The diagram is constructed so that students work through the thinking process of comparison by identifying likenesses and differences, while clearly specifying what the differences "are in regard to." After the introduction of the graphic, the authors suggest that copies of the pages should be readily available in the classroom for students to use for other applications. Although this static map does not demonstrate a highly flexible use of a visual tool (in the sense of students drawing the map on their own), this kind of patterning by students may lead to automaticity with this essential skill and low-road transfer of the process across disciplines.

Several similar teacher resource books and approaches have been developed showing the use of thinking-process maps to facilitate teacher curriculum design and to support students' thinking (Clarke 1991, Fogarty and Bellanca 1991, Marzano 1992). As in the work of Parks and Black (1992), most of these applications present a collection of isolated processes and a range of content applications. The terminology and uses of these thinking-process maps—generically called graphic organizers—generally reflect many of the goals of the thinking skills movement. They are used to focus on facilitative teaching, cooperative learning, transfer of thinking processes to content learning, metacognition, and the construction of knowledge by students. Most of these tools are

effective for what Perkins and Soloman (1989) have called the "low-road transfer" of thinking processes.

In contrast to introducing a disconnected selection of isolated thinking-process maps to students for low-road transfer, several approaches focus on high-road transfer by using a single, flexible, integrated, graphic form to develop students' capacities to synthesize information; construct theories from information; and transfer concepts, propositions, and principles.

One of these maps, developed by John Clarke (1991) and aptly called an "inductive tower" (Figure 5.3), is used by teachers and students to first gather concrete representations of "facts" and experiences and then to synthesize these baseline artifacts into abstract, theoretical propositions. The inductive tower is the counterpart to the use of deductive classification trees, which begin with the general category definition and build down to show members in subcategories. Although this thinking-process map is used across grade levels and as shown in Clarke's 1991 text, *Patterns of Thinking*, the applications range widely across disciplines: from an exploratory science activity in lower elementary, to an interpretation of the poem "The Red Wheelbarrow" by William Carlos Williams, to solving word problems, to troubleshooting a problem in an auto repair class.

The example in Figure 5.3 shows how 3rd graders interpreted the story "The Country Mouse," beginning with factual information from the reading selection, moving up to knowledge claims, and finally to a value position. Clarke's methodology for constructing inductive towers is drawn from Bob Gowin's "Vee" dia-

FIGURE 5.3

Third Grade Inductive Tower

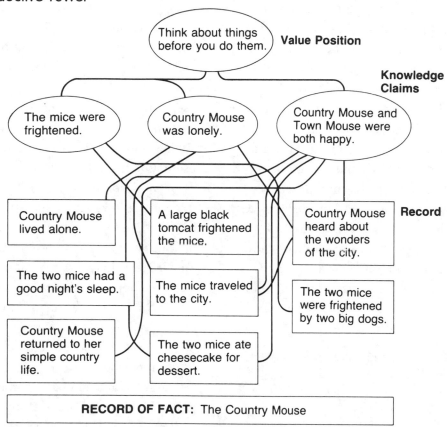

Source: Clarke, J.H. (1991). <u>Patterns of Thinking.</u> Needham Heights, Mass.: Allyn and Bacon. Reproduced by permission.

gram (Novak and Gowin 1984), which presents rising conceptual understandings:

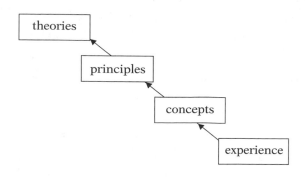

This use of the inductive tower reflects what every reading teacher—and every teacher across the disciplines—would want students to be able to do on a regular basis. This is not simply the identification of the main idea from supporting evidence. From a factual, base level, students must generate midlevel inferences and propositions, and then go on to generalize from these foundations a high-level value statement or prediction.

The use of visual tools for facilitating students' conceptual development may be traced to a significant body of work. Many of the developers of thinking-process maps working in the past dozen years have been influenced, as has Clarke, by the text *Learning How to Learn* (Novak and Gowin 1984). The authors developed a process called "concept mapping" that represents learning as the integrated, hierarchical, and holistic development of interconnected ideas. Based on David Ausubel's theory of learning and his early work using advanced organizers (Ausubel 1978), Novak and Gowin focus on the assimilation of new ideas into the conceptual pattern of students' prior knowledge as expressed in a hierarchical form. Novak and Gowin also focus on the construction of knowledge, the meaningfulness of the learning that is taking place, and the reworking of maps to incorporate new understandings. The authors explain their guiding assumption:

> Because meaningful learning proceeds most easily when new concepts or concept meanings are subsumed under broader, more inclusive concepts, concept maps should be hierarchical. Concept mapping is a technique for externalizing concepts and propositions (Novak and Gowin 1984, pp. 15–17).

The authors use some of the same dynamic, graphic forms used for brainstorming webs. Ovals, lines, and linking words are used and interrelated within an adaptable yet strictly hierarchical structure.

Concept mapping is intended to be used flexibly so that the same content or concept may be represented in multiple configurations. Figure 5.4 shows two (and more) possible versions of the concept of the knowledge area of "living

things." Novak and Gowin (1984) use the term "rubber map" to highlight how subordinate concepts may be reconfigured and understood at a higher level on the map. Though the basic graphic design of this thinking-process map is hierarchical, and thus reflects an overarching classification structure, other thinking processes—such as sequencing, cause-effect and part-whole reasoning, and identification of attributes—are implicitly integrated into the representation using linking lines and key words.

What becomes clear as different thinking-process maps are reviewed is that the graphic design offered by a map developer may reveal an underlying conception of a structure of knowledge. Whereas Novak and Gowin's (1984) concept mapping techniques are based on a hierarchical representation of knowing—which reflects a traditional Western view of the form of knowledge—knowledge could be viewed from a different perspective.

Knowledge could be understood as not hierarchical but as a complex of interdependent feedback "flows." This is exactly what the systems thinking approach and the accompanying visual tools are based on. Systems thinkers believe that our traditional definition of cause-effect reasoning and our basic representations of relationships as static (such as hierarchical theories) do not clearly reflect how systems actually work. Systems thinking requires a dramatic reconsideration about how we perceive, organize, and evaluate our world. The fundamental shift is from the organizational structure often found in schools, which lists or categorizes information, to a structure that shows and models dynamic phenomena.

FIGURE 5.4

Concept Mapping

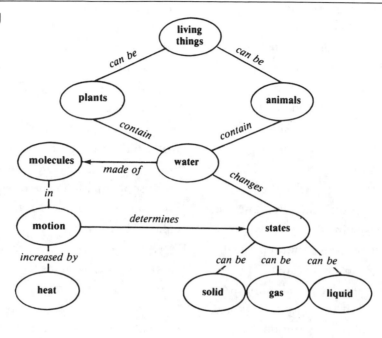

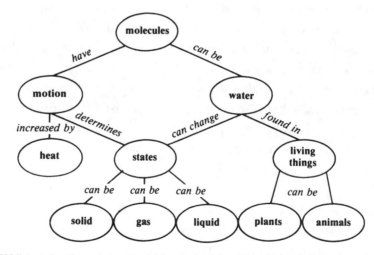

Source: Novak, J.D., and B.D. Gowin. (1984). <u>Learning How to Learn.</u> Cambridge, England: Cambridge University Press. Reproduced by permission.

As a simple example—and systems thinking is simple *if one lets go of linear and hierarchical thinking as sole organizing principles*—here is a concrete example from Peter Senge:

A cloud masses, the sky darkens, leaves twist upwards, and we know that it will rain. We also know that after the storm, the runoff will feed into groundwater miles away, and the sky will grow clear by tomorrow. All of these events are distant in time and space, and yet they are all connected within the same pattern. Each has an influence that is usually hidden from view. You can only understand the system of a rainstorm by contemplating the whole, not any individual part of the pattern (Senge et al. 1994).

One of the first steps for understanding and visually modeling these kinds of systems is to begin sketching feedback loops that represent cyclical interdependencies in a system. The most basic graphic "primitive" used in the systems thinking approach is the feedback loop.

For example, one of most common feedback systems for many of us is the notorious "burnout" syndrome. We may come up with a laundry list of causal factors that feed this condition, but systems thinkers take these factors and show how each relates in a balancing cycle over time. This makes sense because burnout does not happen overnight but over time. Some of the most basic, cyclical, causal relationships in this system are hooked together in feedback loops (Figure 5.5).

As you begin to feel burned out, work starts to seems less important; you have difficulty focusing. Then, as your motivation and focus wane, you get even less work done. But, because you get even less work done, your backlog of things to do swells. As it does, motivation and focus fade even more. And so on. The cycle continues. And, left unchecked, full-blown burn-out ultimately occurs (Richmond, Peterson, Vescuso 1987/1991).

These descriptions—both written and visual—are the basic conceptual building blocks for systems thinking. This is a much different way of perceiving the world than in the normal, one-way flow of cause-effect reasoning; moreover, it is a different way of representing the world than through hierarchical patterns. In the next section we take a closer look at a much more sophisticated view of systems thinking using a set of visual tools activated by software called STELLA.

As we look back over this brief review of thinking-process maps, it becomes clear that many of the developers of these maps are not focused on developing task-specific organizers for content learning, but giving students visual tools that can be used within a discipline, for transferring thinking processes across disciplines, and for interdisciplinary learning. These tools are focused on a much broader set of outcomes: giving students the tools for low-road transfer of thinking processes and high-road understanding and transfer of concepts, principles, and values.

Using Thinking-Process Maps for Individualized, Cooperative, and Schoolwide Learning

Now that we have viewed some thinking-process maps, we may be even more precise about the differences between these tools and task-specific organizers. As you can see, these

FIGURE 5.5

Feedback Loops for Systems Thinking

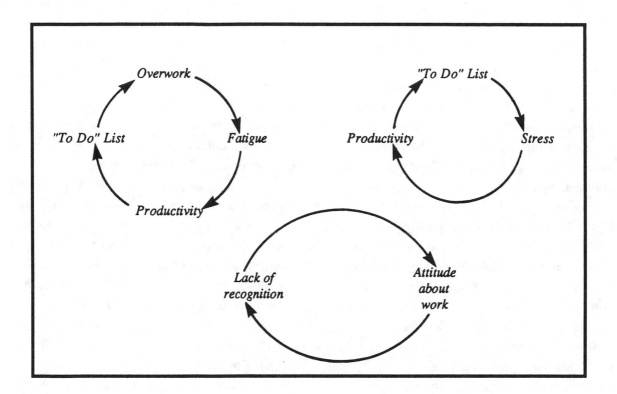

Source: Copyright High Performance Systems. Used by permission.

two types of tools *look* the same. The difference is in how students and teachers interactively use thinking-process maps *over time* for individual, cooperative, and schoolwide learning.

Individualized Learning

Thinking-process maps support individual students' capacities to understand and transfer

their fundamental cognitive processes and to apply these tools to construct and analyze conceptual structures. Once an individual learns how to use thinking-process maps, they become lifelong tools for independent learning and problem solving.

Though the long-term rewards of using thinking-process maps are large, an investment is needed in teaching students flexibility in how and when to use these tools. Unlike the uses of task-specific organizers, which are introduced and defined by a task, and brainstorming webs, which are open ended, students need more detailed instruction, modeling, and follow-up coaching for learning how to use thinking-process maps. Students need such support because they are learning deeply about multiple fundamental thinking processes or more global thinking processes, and then how to manipulate and reconfigure these visual tools to fit learning tasks.

For example, the inductive tower design in Figure 5.3 reveals the visual scaffolding and consistent pathway for understanding and applying the thinking process of developing a concept from a record of facts to a theoretical proposition or value statement. With flexible use and coaching, the individual student has a tool for consciously improving low- and high-road transfer of this theory-building model into every content area and with more complex content knowledge.

Of course, thinking is too complex to be reduced to a few visual configurations. Individual students must develop agility with an array of thinking-process maps so that they may draw on these tools as required by a problem or learning task. This is analogous to a reading teacher's using three or four basic task-specific organizers for focusing students on the multiple tasks for reading a story. Once several thinking-process maps are learned, the ability of the individual to coordinate these tools together with other learning strategies means that complex

problems and processes may be more easily approached and solved. Given an array of maps to choose from, students also have the independent capacity to create their own content-specific applications, much like a teacher who designs several task-specific organizers in response to the learning task.

Though useful for all students, thinking-process maps are especially helpful for those with special needs who have difficulties applying fundamental cognitive processes, constructing concepts, and retaining information. Brainstorming webs, or task-specific organizers that are bound by content areas, may not effectively build students' capacities to consciously apply these processes in different contexts. Organizers are most effective for discrete tasks in certain content areas and implicitly facilitate conceptual understandings, but many students are not able to independently and *consciously* transfer—and thus improve—their underlying thinking processes.

For example, an individual student might have little difficulty in identifying the three major types of rocks and categorizing rock samples within a geology lesson. But that student may have great difficulty identifying major and secondary themes and supporting details in a short novel read in an advanced English literature class. The "contents" of these examples may be different, but the underlying cognitive structure—of hierarchical relationships—is similar. In the first case, the hierarchical structure is based on formal category or taxonomic relationships, whereas the second case may involve informal structures revealing the inclusive hierarchy of ideas linked by an overarching theme. The Tree Map for classifying information shown at the beginning of this chapter (Figure 5.1) or the inductive tower (Figure 5.3) may be used by a teacher in a one-on-one cognitive mediation session with this student to provide a concrete tool for constructing categories.

This low-road transfer of the thinking process *and pattern* of classification into different contexts heightens a student's awareness of a general thought process. An individual student then begins *to see* that this innate process is applied differently across disciplines. The process provides a foundation for high-road transfer and interdisciplinary investigations. This student also begins to take hold of the reins for commanding and controlling her own thinking and for constructing knowledge from basic patterns of thinking.

Cooperative Learning

Many of the ideas noted in the previous two chapters about how to use webbing and organizers for cooperative learning are applicable to thinking-process maps—with one clear distinction. Brainstorming webs are highly idiosyncratic in form, and thus centered more on independent learning. *Task-specific organizers are mostly teacher-centered and can become unwieldy in number as they are designed for each content area.* Conversely, thinking-process maps are fewer in number because there are relatively few, distinct, fundamental thinking processes. In addition, most thinking-process maps are designed with a high degree of flexibility so that students work together to expand each map, as

reflected in the dynamism of analytical and creative thinking. These attributes make thinking-process maps quite useful as collaborative, student-centered tools for communication, group problem solving, and dialogue in cooperative learning formats.

For example, 10th grade students who have become fluent with a range of six to eight thinking-process maps may be assigned to a cooperative learning group and asked to trace the development of the Civil Rights movement from the Civil War to present times. Immediately they recognize that a flowchart, based on the thinking process of sequencing, is an appropriate tool for mapping this development. The simple flowchart is created from rectangles and arrows, but it also might be reconfigured for investigating causal, systems relationships that affected the Civil Rights movement. The students have been coached in transferring this map into different contexts and thus are able to create a configuration that best reflects their knowledge of this topic.

The students begin working together, creating their own multiple-level map. They visually represent not only the efforts of African Americans to gain freedom from slavery, to voting rights and affirmative action policies, but also the efforts of women and other groups who have not been granted full equity and access in the system. As a summary, students may turn to the use of an inductive tower for constructing a new principle from the grounded research they have done in their group.

The outcome of this activity is multifold. Students choose the visual tools that will fit the objective. They also are actively and consciously applying a fundamental thinking process to a complex problem. The teacher is able to move from group to group and assess, at a glance, the developing ideas that otherwise would be invisible. The completed design of the maps then becomes a platform from which the group can conduct further research, predict future events, write a research paper, and present its analysis to other groups. Students also may begin to compare their mental models to those presented by other groups and evaluate their own process and product. Finally, if students from another group have used other thinking-process maps during their investigation, a metacognitive conversation about what kinds of thinking and tools were most effective may raise the learning process to a higher level.

Schoolwide Learning

The long-term implications for using and reinforcing thinking-process maps grade to grade in a whole-school environment reflect many of the core goals promoted by the constructivist-cognitive revolution in general and the thinking skills movement in particular. Given direct training in using these maps, students have concrete tools for independently and interdependently seeking patterns in information. They are empowered to draw on a range of different and related thinking processes, and they are motivated to persevere during complex tasks. They have a well-developed foundation for entering reflective, meaningful dialogue.

As with the other visual tools presented in the previous chapters, a certain amount of con-

sistency in definition and graphic design of thinking-process maps is essential for long-term, schoolwide success. If these tools will be used for continuous cognitive development through the grade levels, students should not be confused by idiosyncratic graphics at every grade level. It makes common sense, and pedagogical sense, that if a schoolwide effort exists for using thinking-process maps, the long-term growth of students should be the focal point.

Practically, students in kindergarten certainly should be introduced to a flowchart based on the thinking process of sequencing and graphically based on rectangles and arrows, followed by a similar visual design through to graduation from high school. This kindergarten student should not go into the next year or classroom to find that the 1st grade teacher requires flowcharts be made with circles and lines with no arrows, followed the next year by the 2nd grade teacher who likes triangles and dashed lines for making flowcharts. *Graphic consistency and definitions of fundamental thinking processes need to be aligned.*

Again, as with task-specific organizers, too many visual tools are visually contradictory as students progress from grade to grade. As suggested in earlier chapters, the whole school faculty may need to share the maps that they use with students and begin to prioritize which maps are most useful and with which design elements. This may be made easier by deciding on a certain set of visual tools that have been piloted and proven effective by other schools, but the first step should be a faculty or curriculum team meeting devoted to investigating which tools are being used by whom and at which grade levels. Another option is to forego the use of isolated thinking-process maps altogether and adopt a visual language, such as the examples of concept mapping and systems thinking diagrams shown in this chapter, or a language of Thinking Maps, as described in the next chapter.

Software for Thinking-Process Maps

As with task-specific organizers, few software programs exclusively based on thinking-process maps are available for students. This may be because brainstorming webs have a longer history, and task-specific organizers are often found in content-specific software programs. Thinking-process maps on software most often are shown in the form of flowcharts for sequencing and tree diagrams for constructing categories. As described in the previous section, MacMapper is a useful set of visual tools on software that presents a blend between task-specific applications and teaching students how to use thinking-process maps.

Thinking Maps software (see "Resources," Innovative Learning Group) is based exclusively on using thinking-process maps for content learning. This software has a tutorial for teaching students thinking-process definitions using Thinking Maps, followed by exercise sets of content area application problems for supporting transfer into different contexts. The Thinking Maps software is highly flexible and responsive, with unique graphics for each thinking process. It is purposefully "tool-based" so that students use the software to work on the content tasks that evolve from within the learning environment. The next chapter describes Thinking Maps software in much greater detail; the chapter is devoted to Thinking Maps as a common visual language for learning.

Both the MacMapper and Thinking Maps software focus on the application of a variety of different thinking-process maps and are used at the elementary as well as secondary levels.

One of the most sophisticated software programs for using visual tools is a systems thinking program called STELLA (Richmond et al. 1987/1991; also see "Resources," High Performance Systems). This program is mostly used in higher education and is only slowly finding niches in secondary schools. Using STELLA in classrooms and businesses requires extensive training. This is because a visual language for systems modeling is being taught along with an alternative way of perceiving and connecting information as well as predicting and assessing change. Systems thinking is actually difficult "to get your mind around" by just talking or writing about it unless one also begins making simple feedback loop diagrams (see Figure 5.5). Systems thinkers seek not only patterns of relationships but interdependencies.

Richmond et al. (1987/1991), the authors of STELLA, describe three basic assumptions within the systems dynamics approach:

• There are positive and negative feedback cycles that influence a system over time, rather than causality that runs one way (from cause to effect).

- The internal patterns of dynamics latent within a system are often *precipitated* by outside forces, rather than that only external causes can "shock" a system.

- Causal factors are interdependent rather than relatively independent.

- Accumulation and flow of information are fundamental to any dynamic process (Richmond et al. 1987/1991, pp. 49–51).

The outcome of systems modeling using STELLA is about mapping these patterns to better understand and predict events within a system, thus seeing how the system might change *over time*.

For example, when a teacher is explaining how a weather system or the human anatomical system or a social system *acts dynamically*, he needs to show long-term effects. Though systems thinking does not require nonlinear visual representations, we are often humbly reduced and constrained by linear communication in our efforts to get these concepts across to students in linear forms. The basic visual tools for creating a STELLA diagram are better understood through the metaphor of the flow of water into a bathtub and out (Figure 5.6).

The rectangle (called a "stock") represents a changing *level* within a system, such as the rise and fall of water in a bathtub. The circles with the "spigots" and arrow represent the *rate* of water flowing into the tub and, on the other side, the rate of water flowing out through the drain. This basic concept of systems thinking may be applied to any system, such as the representation of the dynamics of human population

growth (also in Figure 5.6). An "inflow" of births feeds the population level, and an "outflow" of deaths depletes the population. This is happening at any given time and over time.

To fully comprehend the dynamics of population growth and depletion levels, a systems thinker begins to build a mental model of the essential, interrelated variables that generate births and deaths (Figure 5.7). The rectangles (stocks) in this model are conditions that accumulate over time, such as pollution, levels of economic activity, birth control knowledge, and religious orientations. The circles with the "spigots" on top are the basic rates of "flows" into these stocks. The other circles with curved arrows attached are "converters" that represent variables that affect flows.

For example, the rate of births is mathematically related to the number of couples, the number of children born per couple, and many other factors as shown in this diagram. Each of the stocks and flows is given relative, numerical weights; and the stocks and flows are connected through algebraic equations. This model is thus linked up by a mathematical underbelly so that variables may be changed and the program "run" and tested. Essential to systems dynamics is the attempt to graphically show, mathematically model, and then test predictions of what will happen over time in a system.

All of this might look quite complex, and that is because, in fact, most of our essential questions are not answered simply. Systems thinking cannot be easily understood in this brief description. It is one of the most highly disciplined and possibly most creative forms of

FIGURE 5.6

Isolated Examples of Systems Flows

Water in Bathtub

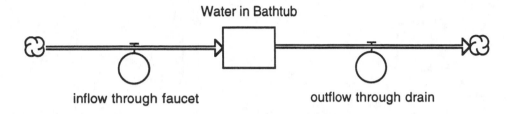

inflow through faucet   outflow through drain

Population

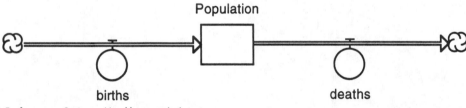

births   deaths

learning: capturing the dynamism of interdependencies through the visual modeling of "systems" rather than collecting isolated "facts" and making assumptions about systems using one-directional, cause-effect reasoning. Thinking from a systems point of view does not require software, but this visual modeling and software are the coordinated tools for deeply investigating systems. We return to a portrait showing how STELLA has been used by students at the middle school level, in the last chapter of this book, which describes how visual tools are key implements for lifelong learning.

Thinking-Process Maps for Assessment

Once students have developed fluency with thinking-process maps, the possibilities for both informal and formal assessment of both thinking and content learning are strengthened. Fluency with these tools is essential because, unlike

FIGURE 5.7

Human Population Dynamics Using STELLA Software

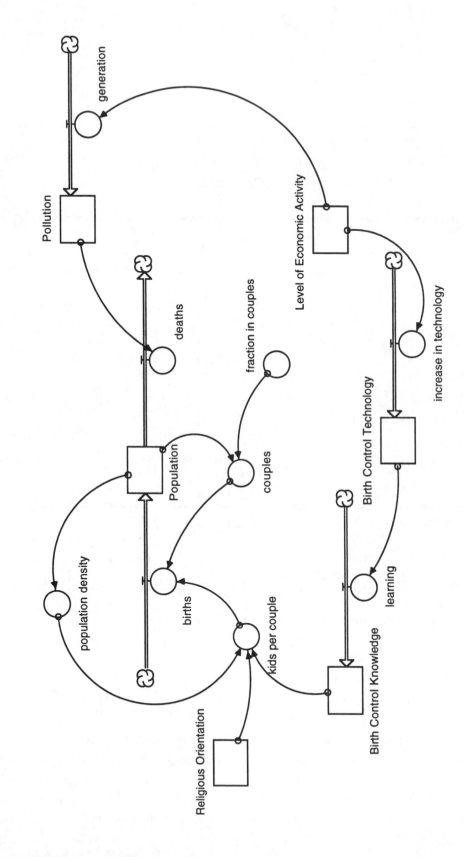

brainstorming webs that are highly idiosyn-cratic in designs and task-specific organizers that are highly structured for content learning, thinking-process maps are based on students' developing conceptual understandings by con-figuring the graphic to the information at hand. This means that assessment is problematic un-less a student has learned how to use each think-ing-process map consistently and flexibly.

For example, after students become fluent with the top-down hierarchical structure of con-cept mapping or the bottom-up inductive tow-ers, we can begin assessing at least two areas: their abilities to construct concepts using these tools and their understanding of concepts that are being taught. One of the general difficulties with using visual tools for assessment is that some students may not be strong visual learners and may dislike, for whatever reason, a particu-lar tool. As with all assessment, we must be care-ful to use multiple means and multiple representation systems for appraising students' work. The most obvious statement of this point is made by Howard Gardner (1983, 1985), who has proposed seven (and possibly more) differ-ent forms of intelligence. Importantly, what Gardner is actually proposing is that intelli-gence may be *represented* and assessed in at least seven different ways, from mathematical representations to interpersonal forms. John Clarke offers some helpful guiding questions for using graphic representations of thinking for the evaluation of individual students:

> Does the graphic really represent what the student thinks? Does it repre-sent how the student thinks? Are there

skills reflected in the graphic that the student may use again? Are there other ways to look at thinking? How much has student thinking changed? What other steps are possible, based on what the student has already done (Clarke 1991)?

All constructions of knowledge by students using visual tools may be filtered through these questions.

Joseph Novak and Robert Gowin (Cornell University) have done the most sophisticated work in the field of assessing learning using vis-ual tools, and in particular using concept map-ping (see Figure 5.4). At a time when the educational community is attempting to bal-ance quantitative measures with qualitative un-derstandings of student work, the concept-mapping approach seems an intriguing entry point into students' understandings:

> Concept maps can be similar to paintings; you either like one or you do not. A simple qualitative judgment of students' concept maps is all that some teachers want. In our early work, we were often asked, "How does one score the children's concept maps?" We were more interested in representing what children's conceptual frameworks looked like before and after instruc-tion, or over a span of years (Novak and Gowin 1984).

This view of concept mapping as useful for qualitative assessment applies to all thinking-process maps, and possibly all visual tools that are student-centered and flexibly used for reveal-ing conceptual understandings.

FIGURE 5.8

Concept Mapping: Scoring Model

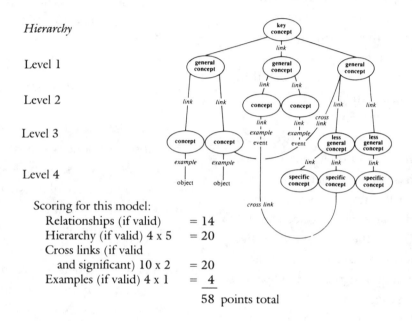

Scoring Model

Scoring for this model:

Relationships (if valid)   = 14
Hierarchy (if valid) 4 x 5   = 20
Cross links (if valid
    and significant) 10 x 2   = 20
Examples (if valid) 4 x 1   = _4_
                                    58 points total

Source: Novak, J.D., and B.D. Gowin. (1984). <u>Learning How to Learn.</u> Cambridge, England: Cambridge University Press. Reproduced by permission.

Nonetheless, these authors and others in this field believe that there are ways of "reading" and "interpreting" students' visually constructed views of knowledge. *Teachers and students must use a relatively consistent graphic design and show fluency with the process, however, before such interpretation is possible.* Novak and Gowin have been successful with a scoring model (Figure 5.8) that is based on three central principles of Ausubel's theory of learning: *hierarchical structure,* which is based on new information being subsumed under more inclusive concepts; *progressive differentiation,* which is the continuous enrichment of concepts as new relationships are constructed; and *integrative reconciliation,* which is based on the synthesis of new and old concepts into new meanings. These principles cannot be fully described in this writing. Translated for our purposes, these three schemes, respectively, focus on the validity of the inclusiveness of ideas, propositional links, and assimilation of concepts.

Whereas these concepts may be scored using the rubric designed by the authors, clearly these three principles can be used separate from concept maps as qualitative guides for coming to understand how a student is constructing and transforming relationships. Importantly, Novak and Gowin suggest that a concept map (or inductive tower or systems diagram) is something that is first envisioned, revised, and finally redrawn by the student so that the map is a centerpiece for a one-on-one conversation between a teacher and the student. In these terms, these maps are actually end products and not merely midrange tools. Of course, no map stands alone. Students need to be able to talk through the map, verbalizing their thinking and engaging in a dialogue about the construction of concepts and knowledge.

Though Novak and Gowin point out that other forms of maps are viable as assessment tools—such as flowcharts, feedback loop diagrams, and predictability trees—they believe that concept maps mirror a clear theory of learning as articulated by Ausubel, which they are convinced reflects in a clearer way the structure of knowledge. This last point is crucial to the use of thinking-process maps for assessment purposes. Once a teacher, researcher, or test maker offers a generative visual *form,* they have to clearly articulate, as have Novak and Gowin, their "view" of knowing and their "view" of the structure of knowledge. This view of knowledge and how it is specifically structured is rarely explicitly articulated in classrooms, schools, districts, or even at the college level. Educators, historically, have presented knowledge as

strictly hierarchical in form. By using visual tools, educators will begin the intellectually rigorous task of displaying their belief systems and different views of various structures of knowledge. Novak and Gowin may believe in the hierarchical interconnectiveness of knowledge; systems thinkers may believe in the dynamic feedback flow of knowledge; and researchers such as George Lakoff (1987) may believe in the metaphorical structure of concepts and knowing.

Each of these forms is powerful when activated as a visual tool for learning and assessing. Together, they present a new *form* for assessment focused on conceptual linkages. Visual model building may, at some future date, surpass other forms for assessing content learning in classroom being used today. Why? First, the process of concept mapping and other forms shown in this chapter are relatively easy to learn and fun to use. Second, regardless of their abilities to verbalize or write down their ideas, students must independently demonstrate their mental models for how all of the information pertaining to a certain topic or interdisciplinary theme is interrelated. Third, concept mapping and other thinking-process maps require that students show holistic, not isolated, knowledge, and this fits the theoretical and practical understandings we now hold as important in the constructivist paradigm. And finally, students will represent their thinking in linear *and* nonlinear ways—which may be much more authentic than representing interrelationships within the traditional linear confines of written, spoken, or algebraic sentences.

Of course, one of the difficulties with the use of any one of these thinking-process maps is that one map is not enough. Our thinking generates many different patterns of thinking, and thus multiple types of maps. The next chapter investigates a *common visual language* of thinking-process maps, called Thinking Maps. This language, or model, is based on eight fundamental patterns of thinking processes. This language of visual tools starts with eight different graphic "primitives" and provides students with the developmental tools that, together, integrate many of the isolated uses of the successful patterns of thinking reviewed in this chapter.

Thinking Maps: A Common Visual Language for Learning

As learners, we thrive creatively and analytically largely because of our capacities for language use and our abilities to manipulate languages in different contexts. We learn alphabets and grammars for our primary and "foreign" languages, numerical systems in mathematics, scientific symbols, musical notation, computer languages, and the graphics of international sign language. Unless used solely for oral communication, most languages are formed from visual "primitives," each with its own consistent design and combined for communication purposes.

Languages are sustained because there is rule governance, redundancy, and inherent flexibility to combine the different primitives into meaningful units that can be easily used to communicate information, ideas, and emotions on a daily basis. Languages change, sometimes die, and new languages emerge. In addition to language use, we also thrive because we create tools that extend our bodies and minds, enabling us to transform the world around us.

In this chapter, we investigate a language of eight interrelated visual tools that enable students to mentally extend their thinking abilities. This common visual language of thinking-process maps, called Thinking Maps, is used by students and teachers alike for communicating and learning across disciplines and grade levels.

In the previous chapters, we investigated three different types of visual tools: brainstorm webbing, task-specific organizers, and thinking-process maps. The uses for these tools sometimes overlap, but each has unique qualities that reflect certain purposes and uses. Each type of tool also has shown effectiveness related to its purposes, whether it be for facilitating creativity, organizing specific content knowledge, or for improving thinking abilities of students. Of these three types of visual tools, thinking-process maps seem most conducive as a foundation for a common visual language for learning.

Brainstorming webs are, by definition and use, idiosyncratic and thus not as appropriate for building a common language. Though Tony Buzan (1979) offers some common guidelines for brainstorming, a common set of graphics for brainstorming can defeat the purpose of each learner developing a personal visual style. Task-specific organizers are most often used as isolated graphics because they are designed to reflect particular content knowledge or specific content areas. Whereas languages could be created from either of these two types of tools, thinking-process maps have a natural base in the integrated relationships of fundamental human cognitive processes.

The previous chapter detailed two examples of languages based on thinking-process maps: concept mapping and systems diagramming using STELLA software. The language of concept mapping is based on a hierarchical form and is used to generate conceptual understanding from graphics made only of ovals, connecting lines, and linking terms between and among graphics. STELLA is a rigorously defined yet highly flexible language that is based on constructing a sophisticated framework of systems feedback flows. The symbols of this language are boxes, spigots, circles, arrows, and clouds. Both of these visual languages exemplify the power of language use: Students and teachers can work closely together using common visual symbols for constructing, communicating, and assessing knowledge. Though both of these languages are theoretically valid and practically useful, they also have constraints in that each relies on a single explicit design for structuring knowledge: hierarchical and feedback-flow systems, respectively.

Thinking Maps, as a comprehensive visual language, is a toolkit of eight basic designs for thinking that includes the capacity for generating hierarchical relationships and simple systems feedback flow. Also embedded in this language is a map for brainstorming contextual information, and many of the maps are easily reconfigured by teachers into task-specific formats for deeper content learning. In addition, when using Thinking Maps, teachers and students use many of the most effective techniques for applying visual tools described in previous chapters.

This common visual language for learning is thus used as a synthesis of many of the visual tools presented in this book, though it certainly does not replace all other visual tools. Thinking Maps have proven to be highly successful in more than 300 whole schools within the United States, as shown by student results on standardized tests, for improvement of holistic writing scores, and in qualitative terms (Hyerle 1995). Yet an important question must be addressed here: Why have a language of visual tools when all of these different types of webs, organizers, and maps are available?

One part of the answer is held within the question itself: Students and teachers are inundated by *all of these differing types* of visuals to the point that inconsistent use and lack of clear definitions may be confusing students' thinking rather than clarifying it. Another part of the answer is that inconsistency in the use of these tools prevents individual students—over their educational lifetime—from ever mastering any of these valuable techniques. A third part of the answer is found in the intellectual rigor of learning a new language as students use a common symbol system for integrating, coordinating, and depicting their ideas.

A last response comes from the field. From the successful use of Thinking Maps in whole schools and districts over multiple years, educators have found that this integration of visual tools is continually challenging, exciting, and fun for students and teachers. Students and teachers don't seem to get bored over time when using this language. One reason for this interest may be that they are learning a new

way of decoding and sharing their own thinking in the classroom and across a school in many different ways. The unflagging interest also may come from the common bond that Thinking Maps offer to a whole classroom, school, or district. This bond is especially evident to those learning communities that have been seeking ways to fully engage and facilitate all students' thinking in inclusive settings.

Thinking Maps

Thinking Maps use a language based on eight simple but expandable graphic forms, each representing a fundamental thinking process. The eight basic Thinking Maps are shown and titled by use within the Circle Map in Figure 6.1. Theoretically and practically, this language is not understood or used in either a linear or hierarchical way. Students and teachers learn to use one or a combination of the Maps as needed in response to a learning objective.

For example, teachers soon realize that any or all of the maps could be used at any level of Bloom's Taxonomy. For students, teachers, and administrators in a whole school who have practiced and become fluent with this language, these eight maps become a natural complement to written and spoken words and numerical symbols, because they represent thinking processes that are accessible to every student and easily transferred across disciplines.

Once students become fluent with the basic Thinking Maps, they are much less dependent on teachers for facilitating their thinking and reflectiveness. Because students gain control of a

FIGURE 6.1

A Common Visual Language: Thinking Maps®

Thinking Maps®

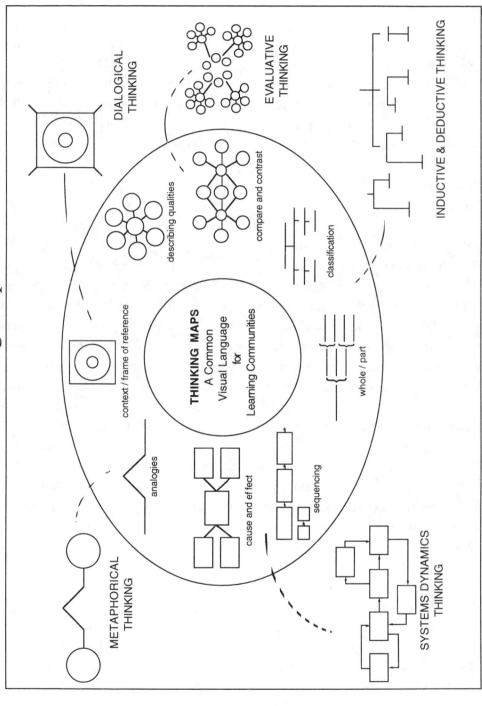

The term "Thinking Maps" with or without the graphic forms of the eight Maps have registered trademarks.

language for expressing their thinking, this flexible vocabulary acts as an array of cues, guides, and reflective questions for prompting students to independently make sense of the world. By introducing a consistent and flexible graphic language to students—one that can be expanded into complex applications—teachers also are providing tools to students for daily communication and dialogue about the form of their ideas.

This consistency and flexibility also supports students as they move from simple to complex content learning and as they mature from novice to expert problem solvers. Within the field of cognitive skills instruction, the present theoretical framework for learning is based on Bloom's Taxonomy (1956). Many educators believe in hierarchical levels of thinking, so-called lower- and higher-order skills. Within the Thinking Maps language, this distinction is made by seeing that higher-order processes are partially extensions from a central core of fundamental thinking processes. Within the frame surrounding the Circle Map (Figure 6.1), you see that one or several of the maps may be combined to form more complex extensions of the basic tools and thus promote different, more complex pathways for thinking and communicating.

For example, the Sequencing and Cause-Effect Maps together support systems thinking and feedback diagramming; the Describing and Comparing Thinking Maps may be used for establishing criteria for in-depth evaluation; the Classification Map leads to theory development similar to the use of the inductive tower shown in the previous chapter and the Tree Map in the Introduction.

Before examining how these maps are used in classrooms, let's first investigate the five essential characteristics of these common visual tools and the definitions of each tool, which together make these tools worthy of being called a "language for learning."

Five Characteristics of Thinking Maps

Every road map has its own key or legend on a corner of the page for reading the signs, symbols, and icons that dot the paper landscape and represent different types of highways, landmarks, towns, counties, and states. Many of these symbols have become universal, which means that information is easily conveyed across cultures. Analogously, a language of visual tools would also have this same characteristic that cartographers use for clear communication: consistent graphics.

Of course, Thinking Maps, like all visual tools, are much more than static displays for filling in information. Because Thinking Maps are used by all learners for constructing knowledge, they need *consistent* graphics as well as the characteristics of being *flexible*, *developmental*, *integrative*, and *reflective*. The following is a summary of the five essential characteristics of this visual language.

Consistent Graphics

Consistency is the hobgoblin of small minds unless it is balanced with a high degree of flexibility. Most languages are inherently consistent, yet flexible. The language of Thinking Maps is constructed of thinking-process definitions and terms, a name for each map that metaphorically reflects the design and use of the map, and eight consistent and flexible graphic starting points, or *graphic primitives* (Figure 6.2).

These graphic primitives are obviously *arbitrary*, just like all other human languages and symbol systems. For instance, there is no clear reason why the numbers one, two, and three have the visual design of 1, 2, and 3. But as people of this common culture, we agree to use these common symbols. If we work without these agreements to common symbols, communication would be nearly impossible. Using the same reasoning, asking everyone to use a Flow Map based on rectangles and arrows, we are agreeing to the use of a common visual language to represent our thinking. Like the Flow Map, each of the other Thinking Maps is based on a unique visual lexicon that reflects a unique thinking process and enables us to share patterns of thinking.

For example, students easily learn from teachers that whenever they are constructing a sequence of ideas, it makes sense that they all start by using a similar graphic starting point, or graphic primitive. They simply begin drawing and expanding the Flow Map using rectangles and arrows, which evolves into different configurations according to how they are individually seeing the information. They *do not* start by drawing out a fully developed map as presented in Figure 6.1. When students construct categories, they also learn to use horizontal, vertical, or diagonal lines. On the most basic level of symbolic representations, as a student or teacher draws every line, circle, or rectangle of a Thinking Map, it represents a decision about the construction of knowledge and is, in essence, cognitively *meaningful*.

Flexibility of Forms

As previously noted, consistency without flexibility creates small minds. The eight Thinking Maps are applied with consistency *and* flexibility. Whereas consistency is based on the graphic form, flexibility is based on students' capacities to expand the graphic and create their own configurations of the map using the common form. This is again analogous to other forms of language: Once students develop fluency with words, phrases, and grammatical conventions, they have the basic tools for writing an infinite variety of letters, poems, short stories, and, possibly, the great American novel.

The student has ultimate control over the developing configuration of the map to reflect the unique, complex ideas being constructed. For example, a Multi-Flow Map for cause-effect reasoning may be expanded in any direction on a page and evolve into a systems diagram showing feedback loops. A Tree Map may be expanded horizontally and vertically, starting from the bottom (inductively) or the top (deductively), to show general to specific relationships. This hierarchical map also may lead to theory development using techniques designed by John Clarke (1991) for using an inductive tower. A Bridge Map for seeing analogies may be extended horizontally or vertically to "bridge" a concept analogically and extend to form a metaphor with multiple levels of relationships.

The flexible and generative quality of each map is essential for students as they engage in both creative and analytical thinking. The linked characteristics of consistency and

FIGURE 6.2

Graphic Primitives and Definitions

primitives	Thinking Maps and the Frame	expanded maps

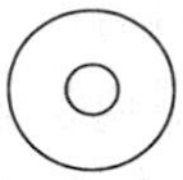

The Circle Map is used for seeking context. This tool enables students to generate relevant information about a topic as represented in the center of the circle. This map is often used for brainstorming.

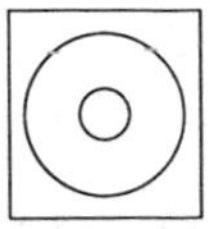

The Bubble Map is designed for the process of describing attributes. This map is used to identify character traits (language arts), cultural traits (social studies), properties (sciences), or attributes (mathematics).

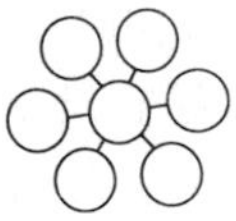

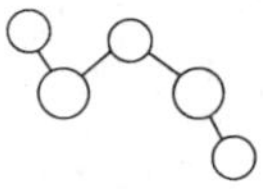

The Double Bubble Map is used for comparing and contrasting two things, such as characters in a story, two historical figures, or two social systems. It is also used for prioritizing which information is most important within a comparison.

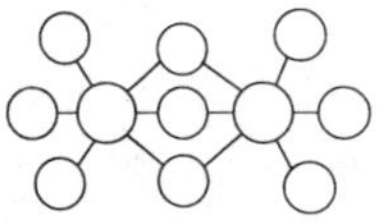

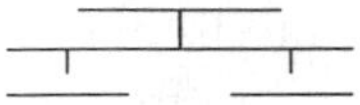

The Tree Map enables students to do both inductive and deductive classification. Students learn to create general concepts, (main) ideas, or categories headings at the top of the tree, and supporting ideas and specific details in the branches below.

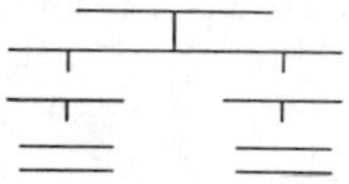

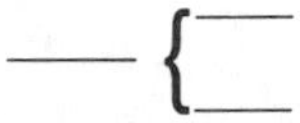

The Brace Map is used for identifying the part-whole, physical relationships of an object. By representing whole-part and part-subpart relationships, this map supports students' spatial reasoning and for understanding how to determine physical boundaries.

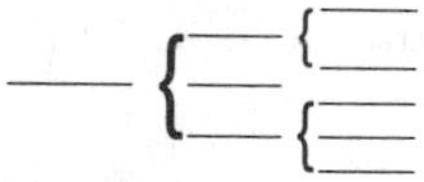

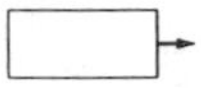

The Flow Map is based on the use of flowcharts. It is used by students for showing sequences, order, timelines, cycles, actions, steps, and directions. This map also focuses students on seeing the relationships between stages and substages of events.

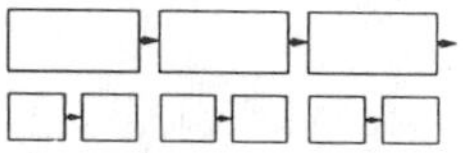

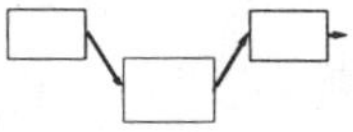

The Multi-Flow Map is a tool for seeking causes of events and the effects. The map expands when showing historical causes and for predicting future events and outcomes. In its most complex form, it expands to show the interrelationships of feedback effects in a dynamic system.

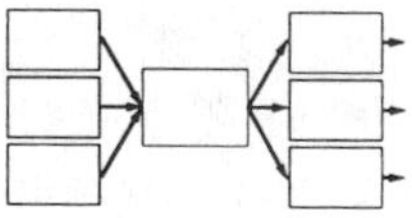

The Bridge Map provides a visual pathway for creating and interpreting analogies. Beyond the use of this map for solving analogies on standardized tests, this map is used for developing analogical reasoning and metaphorical concepts for deeper content learning.

The Frame

The "metacognitive" Frame is not one of the eight Thinking Maps. It may be drawn around any of the maps at any time as a "meta-tool" for identifying and sharing one's frame of reference for the information found within one of the Thinking Maps. These frames include personal histories, culture, belief systems, and influences such as peer groups and the media.

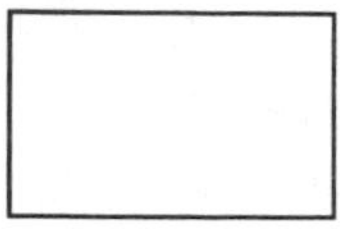

flexibility are most important, of course, because students in cooperative learning groups and teachers working with a whole class are able to think together, share ideas, and synthesize different patterns of information. This is made most effective and efficient because they have a common visual language for seeking interrelationships and for bringing greater clarity to their work.

Developmental Use from Novice to Expert

The most significant outcome of having simple graphic primitives that are consistent and flexible is that learners from preschool through adulthood are able to use the same tools at different levels of complexity. These forms also may be a common set of communication tools for multi-age, inclusive schools.

This common visual language supports the basic needs learners have for continuous cognitive development, from novice to expert uses of fundamental thinking processes. As a learner becomes a more sophisticated, relational thinker using these maps and other strategies and resources, the refinement in the use of the maps also grows. A young child (a novice in applied thinking) may begin developing simple patterns for each map. In later years this child will develop the capacity to construct different configurations of multiple maps for complex thinking (an expert in applied thinking).

For example, using a Flow Map, a kindergarten student may draw, with some guidance, the beginning, middle, and ending events in a story and may add a few words. Six years later, the same student may generate a Flow Map show-

ing the more complex cyclical stages of the evaporation cycle. In college or the workplace, the same student may develop a sophisticated computer Flow Map with an intricate parallel processing format for a design for a new robotics factory.

This example also shows a second benefit: that a novice is able to move from a simple view of one process, such as sequencing, to develop a deeper and differently complex understanding of this process. As shown in Figure 6.2, the Bridge Map for seeing analogies is a tool that can be expanded to another related but differently complex form: conceptual metaphor. Of course, the sophistication of use of these tools is partially related to a student's cognitive growth, content knowledge, the environment in which he or she is learning, and the access to quality educational resources and experiences. Yet if each of the tools is taught to all students to a level of fluency—in any environment—an individual may internalize these tools in a way that this language becomes a self-generating form for continuously improving the capacity to think in school and the workplace.

Integrated and Interdisciplinary Use of Maps

After each of the eight Thinking Maps has been introduced and practiced by students, they are enabled to transfer these tools to content learning: for reading comprehension across disciplines, writing processes, social studies research, the scientific method, and mathematics problem solving. During this transfer process, teachers use sample pages from a training guide (Hyerle 1995) to model transfer and to coach students in using multiple maps (see also "Resources" section of this book). Students and teachers thus become more aware of how to choose which thinking processes (as applied using the maps) are most useful given a specific learning or performance objective.

A common starting point is reading comprehension. A novice reader employs multiple thinking processes and specialized reading strategies to comprehend a story. Several or all of the Thinking Maps may be used for seeking basic text structures. The Bubble and Double Bubble Maps might be used, respectively, to describe and then compare characters in a story. The Flow Map could be used to identify the stages and substages of the plot; the Multi-Flow Map is often used to analyze the causes and effects of actions of a central character. The Tree Map might then be used to synthesize all of this overlapping information into a more concise view of the main theme (or idea), supporting ideas, and details of the story. The Bridge Map may be used to interpret similes and metaphors that guide the generation of symbolism for the piece of writing. These six Thinking Maps could be used by individual students, in cooperative groups, or by the whole class, with the teacher facilitating the construction of the maps and dialogue during this interpretative process.

With practice, students learn to link Thinking Maps together on a single page and sometimes embed one map within another to solve complex problems or to communicate ideas. Moreover, Thinking Maps may be presented to students—depending on the grade level—as common tools in classrooms for integrated in-

struction and for interdisciplinary units of study.

Many interdisciplinary design approaches begin with the identification of a theme that requires students to synthesize content knowledge and conceptual principles from across various disciplines. This design may be further supported by focusing on one or several thinking processes that are required by students for integrating information to form interdisciplinary understandings. In this example (Figure 6.3), the 3rd grade theme of "Time, Change, and Growth" not only focuses on the content concepts, but on the explicit processes of sequencing and cause-effect reasoning, as well as extensions of these processes, cyclical relationships, and systems dynamics, respectively. These thinking processes and extensions are just two of the underlying cognitive processes that are used across disciplines. By activating these thinking processes as patterns developed using Thinking Maps, students are heightening their understanding of the theme and gaining valuable practice in low-road (thinking skills) and high-road (principles) transfer, as described by Perkins and Soloman (1989) in the previous chapter.

Reflectiveness

One of the central concerns of the constructivist-cognitive revolution is the development of students' metacognitive abilities, or "epistemic cognition" (Costa 1991). Through metacognition, students become aware of thinking processes, their own problem-solving strategies, learning styles, and the nature of knowledge,

FIGURE 6.3

Tree Map for Interdisciplinary Design

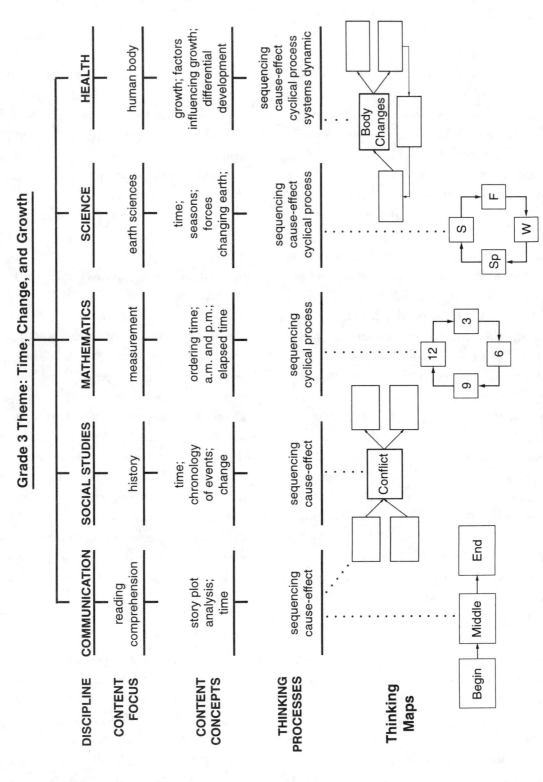

Grade 3 Theme: Time, Change, and Growth

DISCIPLINE	COMMUNICATION	SOCIAL STUDIES	MATHEMATICS	SCIENCE	HEALTH
CONTENT FOCUS	reading comprehension	history	measurement	earth sciences	human body
CONTENT CONCEPTS	story plot analysis; time	time; chronology of events; change	ordering time; a.m. and p.m.; elapsed time	time; seasons; forces changing earth;	growth; factors influencing growth; differential development
THINKING PROCESSES	sequencing cause-effect	sequencing cause-effect	sequencing cyclical process	sequencing cause-effect cyclical process	sequencing cause-effect cyclical process systems dynamic
Thinking Maps					

whether it is received or constructed. The purpose of focusing on metacognitive behaviors is to facilitate students' internal locus of control over their environment and their capacities for self-assessment.

Most of the examples of visual tools shown in this book implicitly, if not explicitly, support metacognitive activity. Even though visual tools make patterns of thinking more accessible, and have been called "displayed metacognition" (Costa in Clarke 1991), no one can guarantee that students will reflect on a visual display any more or less than with other modes of communication. Metacognitive activity often depends on teachers' asking the questions that will facilitate students' reflective thinking.

To "prime" reflectiveness while using Thinking Maps, students are taught how to use a visual cue to elicit their reflections about how they are thinking. A simple graphic, called the Frame, is used as a "meta-tool" with the language of Thinking Maps. This graphic *explicitly* promotes reflectiveness by concretely linking the learner's frame of reference to the construction of knowledge. The Frame is a simple rectangular form that students draw around any of the maps to question and cue the background frames that are influencing their construction of knowledge. This tool reflects a wide array of research in areas such as conceptual metaphor (Lakoff 1987), frame semantics (Fillmore 1986), mental modeling (Johnson-Laird 1983), and mental spaces (Fauconnier 1985). Of course, much of this cognitive research reinforces what any kindergarten or college teacher will tell you: Personal, interpersonal, and social-cultural experiences and belief systems *frame* how students construct knowledge.

In the long term, just introducing students to a common visual language such as Thinking Maps should have significant implications for developing reflectiveness. Ultimately, as a range of consistent and flexible patterns of thinking are introduced, applied, and reinforced, students deepen their understandings of interrelated thinking processes *over time*.

The five characteristics of Thinking Maps are essential to the practical introduction, application, and lifelong use of these tools by students. Educators sometimes raise two concerns when they're introduced to Thinking Maps. One is about the actual selection of the eight thinking processes as the foundation for the maps. This was not an arbitrary decision. As the next section shows, the Thinking Maps language was developed from a comprehensive model of eight *fundamental* thinking processes (Upton 1941/1960, Samson 1975). Cognitive psychologists and educators often disagree about which cognitive processes are "fundamental," but the Upton-Samson model correlates quite clearly to Piaget's identification of basic cognitive processes and to recent cognitive science research. These processes are: representing (in context), describing attributes, comparing, categorizing, part-whole relationships, sequencing, cause-and-effect reasoning, and relational reasoning (reasoning by analogy). A highly theoretical discussion about whether or not these are a complete set of fundamental processes is not appropriate here, but it is clear that Thinking Maps represent a live language and that additional tools can be added at another time.

A second concern raised by the use of any language or model is the risk of reducing a complex array of actions (or thinking processes) to a few simple steps. There is also the fear that communication will be constrained and thinking confined by the form of a language or model. This has happened often in education as we go about implementing a new "model" only to find that, when translated and overly refined, it becomes a rigid, procedural process. You may wish to retain this skepticism as we further investigate this language of visual tools. But also keep in mind those great masterpieces that have been created by poets, composers, and, yes, computer scientists because they and their audiences had *a common language* through which to communicate and discover new ways of understanding.

Background and Implementation Design for Thinking Maps

The Thinking Maps language can be traced back to a semantics-based model of fundamental cognitive processes first developed by Albert Upton, a professor at Whittier College during the 1950s and '60s (Upton 1941/1960). This model, which was modified by Upton's colleague Richard Samson (1975), became the foundation for two K–9 content-based programs: a comprehensive language arts program

called "THINK!" and a basic mathematics program called "Intuitive Math." These materials were later translated into a cognitive skills-based program called "Strategic Reasoning" (Citron and Glade 1985).

In the late 1980s, the "Expand Your Thinking" program (Hyerle 1988–1993) was developed for middle school students, based on the Upton-Samson model. The Thinking Maps emerged during the process of writing this program. What evolved was a transformation of several definitions of thinking processes of the Upton model to reflect current cognitive research and the additional definition of each of the eight thinking processes *as visual tools.* The model of Thinking Maps as a language was further developed as part of a curriculum design guide for educators (Hyerle 1990) and doctoral research (Hyerle 1993). Currently, materials, software, and professional development training manuals are available to implement Thinking Maps using a schoolwide approach (Hyerle, 1991, 1995–96; see also "Resources," Innovative Learning Group).

The design for implementing Thinking Maps in a whole school is structured so that when teachers return from a training workshop to classrooms, they will have the capacities and basic resources to interactively introduce these tools directly to students at any grade level. Ideally, all eight maps are introduced and modeled by teachers over eight weeks and then reinforced using content-transfer activities developed by teachers until students gain automaticity with this language. Teachers would also receive continued follow-up support in classrooms for a minimum of one year—and often over two or three years—as they become expert in using the tools for cooperative learning, curriculum design, and assessment.

Because all teachers in an elementary, middle, or high school are trained, students have reinforcement for applying these tools as they move from grade to grade or classroom to classroom. Students learn incrementally, and over time, that this is an interrelated language, or set of tools, not just eight separate thinking-process maps. The implementation design is also based on a high degree of interactive teaching and paired and cooperative learning so that students use these maps as collaborative tools from the first. Most importantly, the intended outcome of this professional development approach is not for teachers and students to go through exercises in a program, but to learn how to use a common visual language for learning as they develop lifelong habits of mind.

Thinking Maps for Integrating Individual, Classroom, and Schoolwide Learning

Thinking Maps are almost always introduced to students, teachers, and administrators on a schoolwide basis. Essentially, the whole faculty learns a new language that is fully integrated into and transforms the learning environment. This whole-school training supports consistent, flexible, and developmental use of Thinking Maps for integrating individual, cooperative, and schoolwide learning. The implementation design consists of training whole school faculties over the course of a year in how to use these tools for interactive teaching, cooperative learning, content-specific transfer, integrated learning, and assessment.

Individual Learning

After students have been introduced to each Thinking Map using an integrated sequence of eight short lessons leading to a self-concept writing assignment, they are coached by teachers on how to apply the Maps to content-specific and interdisciplinary learning. A poster set is displayed in front of the classroom showing each of the eight Maps for easy reference. Though students soon recognize that they are responsible for ownership and use of these tools, teacher modeling, questioning, and cueing of the Maps is essential as students (and teachers) are in the first stages of learning the language.

The learning curve for this introductory process is quite sharp, because each of the Maps relates to questions that teachers regularly ask, such as "How would you describe this character?" and "How are these characters similar and different?" This introductory learning phase consists of using only one or two maps at a time. For example, a teacher may model how to use the Bubble Map for identifying character traits and then ask students to work in pairs on creating Double Bubble Maps to compare two characters from the story. As use of the tools is repeated over time, teachers and students (depending on the developmental level) begin linking multiple maps together in response to the complexity of the work at hand.

The outcomes for the individual learner can be reduced to a simple phrase: *All students gain ownership of a set of new tools for their minds.* As an individual learns each map, both control of thinking and creative applications emerge, and students develop an internal locus of control rather than depend on the teacher for guidance. Fewer students ask "What do I do?" because they have eight cognitive pathways for actively responding to a question.

Many of the 15 intellectual dispositions highlighted by Art Costa (1991) are facilitated: patience, precision, problem finding, enjoyment of problem solving, and perseverance. Within the first year of learning this language—again, depending on the grade level—students need guidance and modeling for how to decide which Thinking Maps to use, when, and for what outcome. As fluency develops and as their experience grows, students use Thinking Maps as midrange tools for creating final products, such as written or oral reports.

Cooperative Learning

The individual development of the Thinking Maps language is also facilitated by the immediate use of the maps for paired and cooperative learning formats. Because all students are using a common visual language, students work together to construct maps on the way to a final product. Many of the techniques for supporting Thinking Maps in cooperative groups are similar to those described for using other visual tools in the previous chapters.

One new technology that has been successfully piloted for facilitating learning in groups using the maps is a set of eight "Desk Maps." Each of these desk-size, laminated boards have one of the eight graphic primitives on one side and an open workspace showing all eight maps on the other side. A typical class is broken out into eight groups of three or four students, each with a Desk Map. Students are given water-based, erasable color pens for drawing out applications. The teacher may assign each group to approach a given problem or prompt using the Thinking Map they were given or ask them to use the open-ended workspace for choosing and using several maps to work through an assignment.

After groups have completed their maps, several effective options are available. First, the Desk Maps may be rotated from group to group so that all students may see how different groups worked through a problem. Second, each group may stand up and present its application to the class using the visual support of the Desk Map for conveying its work. Third, after these presentations, each group may erase parts of its maps and rework the structures of its ideas given the new information and perspectives of the other groups. Finally, these eight Desk Maps, colorfully filled with multiple maps, may be displayed in the classroom or hallway for continuing reference, further analysis, and communication of knowledge to other learners in the schools.

Schoolwide Learning

During the first year of implementation of this new language, the Thinking Maps begin showing up in many different places. Students' colorful maps are displayed in the hallways and in the main office. The physical education teacher conveys the rules of a game using the Tree Maps; the special education teacher works closely with a blind student in communicating through a Braille Brace Map for spatial relationships. The assistant principal asks a student who has been sent to the office for a behavioral problem to map out the causes and effects of the conflict using a Multi-Flow Map. The principal as supervisor coaches a teacher in a post-observation, and the discussion turns to how students use Thinking Maps in cooperative groups for completing a research project.

During the first weeks of the second year of using Thinking Maps, students, teachers, and administrators across a whole school begin to experience the long-term implications of having a common visual language for learning. In the previous year, they learned the language. Now, a 3rd grade teacher has a new classroom of students, and they all have applied most if not all of the maps to learning. A typical situation occurs: The teacher asks students to compare two presidents as described in a reading selection, and students raise their hands and offer, "We could use the Double-Bubble Map." The teacher now realizes that many of the students have internalized the maps to the point where they are choosing appropriate maps for stated objectives. It will still take more reinforcement, modeling, and practice by students to gain a level of automaticity with the Thinking Maps language, but the long-term possibilities of students' continuous cognitive development and student-centered, independent thinking

are now in sight. *These possibilities exist only because the Thinking Maps have been implemented through the whole school and used across disciplines.*

Of course, in the life of a school, the greatest long-term effect of Thinking Maps may not be on the students but on the teachers and administrators whose personal and professional relationships create the character of the school. There is more than enough evidence to show that teaching is an isolating profession and that the structure of the school day and year does not invite collaboration. This isolation is particularly true at the secondary level, where content distinctions also create walls between teachers. The Thinking Maps, as a common language for learning, provide a communal platform for collaboration in a school. Across grade levels and disciplines, teachers are enabled to share ideas more easily because they have a common focus on thinking-process instruction that is practical, authentic, and student centered.

Software for Thinking Maps

Other than word processing programs, most software that students use in schools is content based. As we have seen in this book, using visual tools for networking information within a computer environment is a highly complementary activity. Of course, visual tools software must be readily responsive to the networking capacities of students' minds.

Thinking Maps: Software of the Mind (see "Resources," Innovative Learning Group, in press), is a new tool-based program developed by Gray Matter Software that directly reflects the five key characteristics described previously for this common visual language. The graphic representations include a consistent lexicon for each map and a high degree of flexibility in expanding the graphics. This software is uniquely suited for interdisciplinary work because students learn to use these tools across disciplines and not as specifically grounded in only one subject area.

Developmentally, students from the mid-elementary grades to the workplace may use these tools at different levels of expertise. They also may use them at increasing levels of conceptual complexity. This software, as with the hand-drawn Thinking Maps, also includes the cueing of students' reflective capacities by showing the Frame around each map for reflective, metacognitive notes. Using Thinking Maps in a computer environment gives students a consistent graphic framework for systematically sorting through, organizing, and reflecting on the stream of information available in cyberspace.

As discussed in previous sections on software for visual tools, all of this must happen quickly, because these tools are highly generative. The software program must be responsive to the rapidly developing thoughts of the user.

For example, a student in 3rd grade who is studying the part-whole relationships of a rose may begin by identifying which thinking process and tool will be most appropriate for analyzing its features. After selecting the map icon from the menu at the top of the screen for the Brace Map for part-whole reasoning (Figure 6.4), the student proceeds to configure the map

according to the major parts of the rose. By the end of this phase of the analysis, the student has also added some subparts of the rose and identified the rose as being part of larger object, a rose bush. But this analysis is not over and may require teacher facilitation, because the student map reveals a misconception about the structure of a single rose. Each individual rose does not have an independent root system as shown on the screen.

Along with an initial tutorial for learning how to efficiently use the Thinking Maps software, students are given exercise sets for each of the eight maps. These sets are used to develop flexible use of the maps on software. The exercise sets also facilitate the transfer of Thinking Maps across content areas and grade levels and the capacity to transform information in multiple pull-down windows. Each exercise requires students to manipulate a map in a different way in response to a problem and then pull down a "writer's window" to write about the work completed in the map and reflect on the thinking processes they are learning about. This sequence—from content problem, to map making, to writing, to metacognitive response—patterns for students the global processes of problem solving. Once the tutorial and exercise sets are completed, the software is used as an open-ended tool for transferring Thinking Maps to content-specific learning and interdisciplinary themes.

While this software is in its first year of piloting in any given class, there are many interesting, long-term implications for this technology in whole schools and districts. Students will become fluent with Thinking Maps much more

FIGURE 6.4

Thinking Maps: Software for the Mind

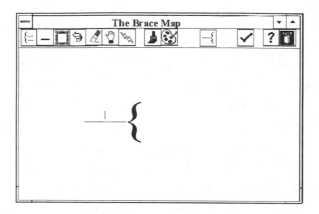

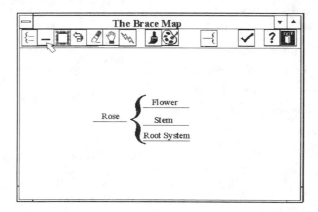

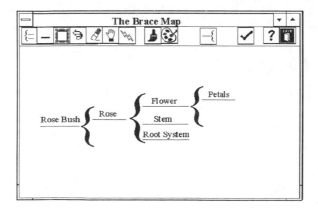

quickly with reinforcement in a classroom computer station or computer lab. The linkage between classroom work and the computer lab also will be strengthened. Moreover, students will be able to share their mental representations of content concepts with ease with other students. Teachers will be able to create learning plans and larger curriculum units with Thinking Maps embedded into the design. They will be able to share these new designs—each with a common cognitive base—with colleagues in their school and district.

Yet the most important dimension of this software is in the area of assessment of students' thinking and content knowledge. Thinking Maps that are collected on disk will become essential documentation of an individual's intellectual growth. Students may also be able to compare their maps to those constructed by other students and be able to compare different styles and conceptions of knowledge. In the long term, students (and their teachers) will have an efficient and in-depth record of how, over time, they have expanded their abilities to think across disciplines.

Assessment Using Thinking Maps

Thinking Maps foster dialogue and reflection by students about their growing content understanding. From a teacher's point of view, students' maps afford both a formative and summative view of their thinking. Thinking Maps offer multiple ways to assess student thinking. Four forms of assessment have been used in schools that have implemented Thinking Maps: pre- and post-instruction measures of students' thinking about a given topic or concept; student inter-

views or conferences; student self-assessment; and as artifacts in a student's portfolio.

Pre- and Post-Instruction Measures

By examining Thinking Maps made by students before and after instruction, teachers can document growth in students' abilities to clarify, expand on, and remember specific content and concepts. The Maps enable teachers to discern whether or not students are:

- increasing their use and variety of details,
- discarding irrelevant and unsupported information,
- expanding the number and complexity of links between disparate pieces of content information,
- making cross-discipline connections,
- integrating previously known with new information,
- making novel applications,
- generating creative ideas, and
- considering multiple perspectives.

Many teachers use the K/W/L format for finding out what students know (K), what they don't know (W), and what they are curious about learning (L). The Thinking Maps provide teachers and students with concrete tools for deepening this process: for seeing students' prior knowledge and then comparing this baseline to Thinking Maps that have been created by students at the end of the instructional unit.

Student Interviews

Metacognition is the ability to formulate a plan of action, monitor progress as the plan unfolds, identify any gaps in thinking or understanding, detect and recover from error, thoughtfully evaluate actions taken, and learn from experience through reflection (Costa 1991). One important method of gauging students' metacognitive abilities is to ask them to think out loud. One-to-one interviews help determine the level of self-confidence, consciousness, and flexibility that students bring to their own learning. Thinking Maps provide a vehicle for discussion and a tangible portrait of how students are relating and connecting information. When a student brings one or several Thinking Maps to the conference, he or she provides a visual representation of thinking. Maps provide the opportunity to both discuss the quality of this thinking as it applies to the construction of knowledge and to set new goals for learning.

Self-Assessment

Student self-assessment promotes personal responsibility for learning, encourages questioning and reflection, and develops respect for the processes required for lifelong learning. By examining their own work against the clear set of characteristics embedded in the Thinking Maps, students can evaluate the developing quality of their thinking. With teacher mediation, students will adopt a developmental perspective on learning. They can review the Thinking Maps in their portfolios, reflect on their strengths and areas for growth, and then use the Maps as the foundation from which to develop new learning goals.

Portfolios

By including Thinking Maps in students' portfolios, teachers capture the development of students' thinking abilities during the course of the school year. Teachers can look for the sustained use of various thinking strategies, as well

as improvements in the students' control over their learning. Teachers can assess students' abilities to use Thinking Maps and thinking processes as the subject matter increases in difficulty, determining whether students are able to perform low-road transfer of thinking processes and high-road transfer of principles and concepts to new learning situations. Of course, one of the difficulties with portfolio assessment is the establishment of a valid system for scoring and evaluating student work. We conclude this chapter with a rubric developed for viewing students' application of skills for lifelong learning.

MAPPER Holistic Scoring Rubric

At this time, in the Information Age and within a constructivist-cognitive mindset, educators are showing an interest and a need to begin gaining much deeper insights not just into *what* students know, but into *how* they are integrating information and constructing knowledge. Given a common and highly flexible visual language for representing ideas and concepts, such as Thinking Maps, we may begin to holistically assess students' growth in their capacities to think through content to final products and performances.

Holistic scoring was first systematically used in schools during the early 1980s as a more standardized way to assess students' writing. Now holistic scoring is used successfully statewide in many parts of the United States. This model blends both qualitative and quantitative forms of evaluating students' sophistication of ideas, organization and support of these ideas using written language, and the particulars of language usage. It is because we have a consistent and highly flexible set of grammatical rules for writing that holistic scoring is needed and possible. This same general process is applied here to students' qualitative growth in thinking and learning.

Assessment using visual tools and mental models is difficult, if not impossible, unless a common language through which all students may communicate is used. And the process must be holistic because it reflects the generative designs of thinking. As presented in the previous chapter, Novak and Gowin (1984) have created a holistic scoring rubric for assessing students' concept maps. Novak and Gowin provide the three theoretical foundations that are used for a holistic scoring rubric for assessing students' conceptual growth of ideas using Thinking Maps: clarifying, expanding, and assimilating (Figure 6.5). Each of these areas is essential for conceptual growth. These three areas are also worthy filters for looking at how students—once they have become fluent with Thinking Maps—construct their ideas for completing final products, or for evaluating performance objectives.

The holistic scoring rubric called **MAPPER** is based on the level (Minimum to Reflective) at which students are applying their thinking processes to content learning (Figure 6.6). Once a Thinking Maps Learning Portfolio has been revised at the end of a school year, the teacher and student sit down and review the documents with this rubric as an informal guide. The portfolio may include projects, selected pieces of writing, and other forms reflecting student performance. Many though not all of these documents would include the use of multiple Thinking Maps that demonstrate how students

generated and organized their ideas to construct a final product.

While systematically scanning the entire portfolio, certain levels of performance may be *observed*. At the lower levels (Minimum to Attending), students are demonstrating a relatively simplistic understanding of the content (rote recall of "the facts") and have not actively transformed the information into a unique product. At the middle level (ParticiPating), students have created integrated Maps of the content, most frequently shown by unique patterns of information and conceptual depth. The higher levels (Effective and Reflective) are demonstrated by students' final products that reveal novel applications and reflectiveness on the process. This rubric has not been systematically piloted by teachers in classrooms, but it has given many teachers an informal structure for gauging the effectiveness of the Thinking Maps and an alternative way of assessing how students are thinking through content.

Each of the previous four chapters has ended with a look at visual tools for assessment. The area of assessment using visual tools should be approached cautiously, but we must also begin to experiment with new ways of "getting into the mind" of students as they are constructing knowledge and not just look at the end-products of their thinking. Visual tools and visual languages are practical ways for seeing the midrange work that students do between the learning assignments we give them and the

FIGURE 6.5

Tree Map of Assessment

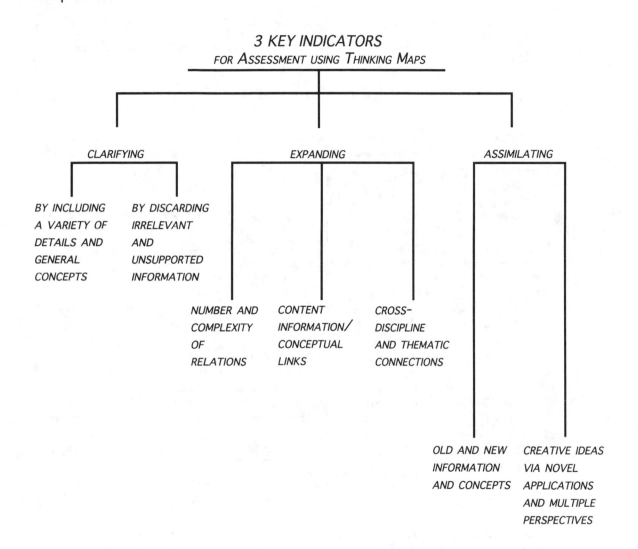

3 KEY INDICATORS
FOR ASSESSMENT USING THINKING MAPS

CLARIFYING

EXPANDING

ASSIMILATING

BY INCLUDING A VARIETY OF DETAILS AND GENERAL CONCEPTS

BY DISCARDING IRRELEVANT AND UNSUPPORTED INFORMATION

NUMBER AND COMPLEXITY OF RELATIONS

CONTENT INFORMATION/ CONCEPTUAL LINKS

CROSS-DISCIPLINE AND THEMATIC CONNECTIONS

OLD AND NEW INFORMATION AND CONCEPTS

CREATIVE IDEAS VIA NOVEL APPLICATIONS AND MULTIPLE PERSPECTIVES

end-products we expect. If, somehow, students can access and show their midrange thinking, we will be able to more effectively assess and, in turn, facilitate our students' thinking. In the next chapter, we examine what this means for students as lifelong, self-reflective learners.

*

Holistic Scale for Assessing Thinking Maps—MAPPER

	Minimum	Attending	ParticiPating	Effective	Reflective
EXPAND	• very few connections • use of only one map	• multiple connections • few supporting details are shown	• multiple concepts are shown with details • multiple Maps are used	• thematic and interdisciplinary connections are shown	• personal, interpersonal, and social implications are recorded
CLARIFY	• bits of information are isolated, disorganized • irrelevant information is included	• different kinds of information are provided • details are shown in relation to general concepts	• patterns in Maps are developed • details are sorted • general concepts are fully supported with relevant details	• connections are shown between multiple Maps • central ideas are highlighted for application	• frame is used to establish point of view and value of Map • hypotheses are generated
ASSIMILATE	• one perspective or solution is shown • rote repetition of information is presented	• alternative way of presenting information is initiated • points of confusion are highlighted	• integration of prior knowledge and new information is shown • fundamental misconceptions are resolved	• several Maps are coordinated for use in final product • novel applications are created	• multiple perspectives are shown • limitations of Map(s) are suggested • self-assessment is initiated
DESCRIPTION	The student is demonstrating a simplistic level of understanding of content and/or limited effort.	The student is attending to the task and demonstrates a basic grasp of content and information.	The student is actively engaged with thinking about content and is beginning to integrate and initiate new ideas.	The student is strategically synthesizing information with a focus on organizing central ideas and details for meaningful applications.	The student is seeking a deeper understanding of knowledge by recognizing multiple interpretations, implications, and limitations of work.
	1	2	3	4	5

Visual Tools for Lifelong Learning

During a recent introductory workshop on using visual tools for student learning, a superintendent raised her hand, stood up excitedly, and showed everyone a document she had just gotten back from the printer. It was a flowchart she was ready to distribute across the district, and it showed the multiple and alternative steps teachers could take to gain professional development units for advancement up the career ladder. She then mentioned that she used hierarchy diagrams to clearly show administrative staff members' levels and interrelationships of responsibility and that the buck stopped at the top, with her.

By this simple example, we see that the visual tools described in this book are not just the latest fad, but well-honed and tested extensions of strategies that we have used in a matter-of-fact way for a long time. These are communication tools that—when reinforced all through the school years—can be used by students who will work well into the next century in over a half-dozen different jobs before they retire. These students must be prepared to become lifelong "relearners." As Alvin Toffler has stated, "The illiterate of the future are not those who cannot read or write, but those who cannot learn, unlearn, and relearn."

We started the first chapter with a portrait of Norm Schuman, a teacher who is a clear example of how just one hierarchy diagram can become a central organizing tool for a 6th grade classroom assignment. This portrait led into a summary of needs that are driving the use of visual tools: constructivism, visual technologies, and interactivity. In this final chapter, we return to these areas through two more portraits. The first is a middle school classroom where students use the software STELLA (see "Resources," High Performance Systems) to diagram systems dynamics. The second portrait shows an elementary school principal who has slowly and surely led the implementation of a common visual language in her school.

These portraits summarize and exemplify how visual tools are used in schools to integrate teaching, learning, and assessment. They also reveal how students' in-depth use of these tools can provide them with the lifelong ability to learn and relearn as they leave school and enter the world of work.

A Portrait of Thinking Through Systems

It was a Monday morning in the spring of 1990 when I arrived at Orange Grove Middle School, just above the recent sprawl of downtown Tucson, Arizona. I recognized the typical modern, single-level, campus design with separate buildings connected by a labyrinth of rain roofs. I had decided to visit when I learned that

Orange Grove was one of the few schools in the United States attempting to use "systems thinking" schoolwide and that the science teacher, Frank Draper, was a linchpin in this effort.

I located Frank's room a few minutes into the first period. As I approached the door, I heard lots of noise inside. Having taught middle school, my first thought was that the kids were out of control; Frank had probably stepped out to find me. But the noise I heard was actually the bustle of conversations between junior high students in twos and threes in front of their computers. They didn't break stride in their work as I entered, but continued to point to their screens and type on the keyboards. I looked for Frank, but what caught my eye was a long ribbon of white computer paper tacked on the front wall. In a dot-matrix, bold typeface, it proclaimed:

THE SIGNIFICANT PROBLEMS WE FACE CANNOT BE SOLVED AT THE SAME LEVEL OF THINKING WE WERE AT WHEN WE CREATED THEM.

—ALBERT EINSTEIN

In the next moment, a teacher came from across the room to greet me. She introduced herself as Deborah, a part-time teacher who was hired to cover classes so that Frank and other teachers could have release time for professional work. She said that Frank often used this period between 8:30 and 10:15 for programming systems models for students to work through. He was in another room and would be back in a few minutes. To my right, three students sat in front of a computer screen, and I asked Deborah what they were doing.

She explained that they were working on a systems program created by Frank. It modeled a proposed natural parkland in African open spaces. The students were experimenting with the variables that affect interdependencies in a dynamic system, such as the environment, wildlife populations, and plant life. The students were to make a mission statement about how the park would be managed, supported by three possible models for how the dynamics of the system would play out over time. This activity would prepare them for producing two environmental issue reports of their own choosing as semester assignments.

A student called out for Deborah, and she left me on my own. I looked around again and noticed another dot-matrix sign tacked on the wall:

Expect to get it wrong and then to learn by figuring out why and fixing it, rather than just getting it right the first time.

That made some sense, but it also conflicted with the common classroom and test expectation that students "get the right answer" immediately.

I took a seat with three students sitting in front of a color monitor. With one hand on the keyboard, Joanne began pointing to the array of bar graphs, pictures of animals, and numbers on the screen. A few feedback loop diagrams were scratched onto a page in front of her.

After quick introductions, I asked Joanne and her classmates what they were doing.

"Well, we are starting with herbivores, predators, and foods. We've got a population of 2,500 total of the animals. And in this park we've got—let's see—okay—let's make this mostly grasslands." At this point she looked down at the keyboard and punched in "grasslands" to establish the environment. The other two students kept their eyes on the screen, suggesting and observing the changes. "Now, we also have lifespans for the different species . . . and somehow we have to balance this out so that the herbivores have enough food and all of the herbivores are not all eaten up by the predators. Oh, yeah—you can also create new kinds of species by putting together parts of each animal. You know, like you can have the top of one with a kind of a jaw for eating meat with the bottom part of another—like a sleek animal."

Joanne created such a predator-monster and put it into the system environment. Then, with a few additions by her labmates, she ran the model to show what might happen over time with the influence of an additional number of these predators. The graph showing the population of these predators went way up as the number of herbivores went way down. After awhile, the ecosystem crashed. Too many predators in the system and not enough meat to eat led to their demise—but only in the long run.

Joanne's response was: "Well, that didn't work. You're about always wrong. Let's try something else."

By this time, the three students at the table next to us were more interested in our conversation than in what they were working on. One boy asked why I was visiting, and I said that I wanted to know if the kind of work they were doing here was any different from what they did in other classes. And then I turned this into a direct question: "Is this any different?"

His response was immediate and as direct as my question: "In the old school we had books and worksheets, now we are doing something. We learn more because we are more interested."

And then Joanne piped up: "Yeah, without the computer, we couldn't be doing this—you know, the calculus."

Finally, Frank returned. He seemed a bit shy, even reticent. He teaches in a well-supported school with additional grant monies and backing from Apple Computers and High Performance Systems, the developers of the STELLA software.

After describing my visit so far, I asked with curiosity: "How do you do all of this? How do you decide what to teach?"

His answer was remarkable in its simplicity: "Instead of only saying to myself, 'What am I going to teach?' I say 'The students are going to help me decide that.' The issue is empowerment."

Frank went on to describe that the students—and the other teachers at Orange Grove—actually do not build many models until they have had experience with manipulating models such as the African ecosystems. They must learn how a wide range of variables influences interdependent systems. The students I observed were working on a pre-existing palette of variables in a system that they could draw from and test. Once they are comfortable with the basic tools that they have practiced—and un-

derstand feedback cycles—Frank introduces the class as a whole to the visual modeling process.

I asked Frank how students responded to this approach. His answer was to the point: He perceives his classroom as a highly interactive place where scientific thinking and research happens, where content is used and tangents are discussed, and where there is a lot of thinking about decisions that are being made, along with the implications for these decisions on systems. In a sense, the class is seen as a system where students are confidently relearning from their mistakes.

Later in the morning, we met with the principal to discuss the implementation of systems thinking and the use of the STELLA software. She immediately revealed her enthusiasm and support for systems thinking, along with a glimpse of the shift the whole faculty had made: "Of course, the staff will have to decide how to proceed, but it has become *not okay* at Orange Grove to look at curriculum as a laundry list."

She explained that this view of the school as a system and curriculum as dynamic was not being presented as a top-down threat or mandate. It was a statement of the realization that the paradigm for how thinking, knowledge, and learning were being defined and practiced was shifting in this school, as all participants gained new understandings about systems thinking. With this movement was a connected shift in how the curriculum was perceived and reconstructed. No longer could curriculum be so easily understood as disconnected content areas that students needed "to cover." From a systems approach, curriculum is not merely a scope-and-sequence list of things to be learned at every grade level. It is a vision of connected content problems and processes that students work through interdependently.

After a long discussion, Frank took a final turn. He suggested that if this paradigm shift toward having students seek interconnections and interdependencies in systems were happening, the old assessment methods would no longer work at Orange Grove. The teach-and-test method with one-shot answers was easily measured. What was needed now were more authentic ways of evaluating what students were doing—something like having a portfolio of students' models to see how they improved over time.

A Portrait of Organizational Change and Continuity

It is time for morning announcements at Joe Hall Elementary School in Miami, Florida. The principal, Barbara Bell, remembers a time when she knew the name of every child in her school. Now she has sketched out what she is going to say to more than 1,400 students. The school site has been slowly expanding over the years, with portable classrooms extending from the main building.

As Barbara steps up to speak, she is aware she will be communicating to a student population that is over 90 percent Hispanic, many having entered Joe Hall with Spanish as their only language. This morning's announcements in-clude, among other things, the step-by-step procedures for early dismissal for the next day and new data that have been collected on the number of student tardies. In addition to being heard over the public address system, she will be seen by the whole school on closed-circuit television.

The Pledge of Allegiance is read, and a student creatively presents the cafeteria menu. Barbara then begins with a welcome to the new day and presents a Flow Map on chart paper. It shows the major steps in the dismissal process. All the students and teachers at Joe Hall immediately know the symbols of boxes and arrows as cues to sequencing information. They have used this and other Thinking Maps over the past two years in all subjects in all grades. Each student has probably used the Flow Map for analyzing the plot of a story, the key events in a history passage, the steps in a mathematics problem, or the procedures for conducting a scientific experiment. As Barbara describes the steps, she points to the different boxes and arrows that are a visual guide for students and teachers.

Barbara then turns to a graph showing the number of tardies schoolwide over the past month. Students in every classroom have collected, tabulated, and graphed the data for their room for every month and sent the results to the front office. Barbara was now presenting the monthly results. This is just one graphical display that has been used as a part of the Total Quality Management (TQM) approach that the whole faculty has been working with for the past few years. The numbers look good; and as she closes her short presentation, Barbara compliments the students not only on their actions in bringing tardies down but also in becoming a part of the solution to this problem.

When the Thinking Maps were introduced to the Joe Hall faculty two years ago as a common visual language, they had already been using several of the TQM transformation tools. They had already begun developing writing process portfolios the year before. Some years before that, the faculty was trained in the assertive discipline program, and through that process they developed their own common, schoolwide guidelines. And even earlier, Joe Hall Elementary School had initiated the core knowledge approach as one of several ways of establishing continuity in content-specific learning across the grade levels.

Significantly, all of these approaches—which run the gamut from traditional to progressive—have been woven together to create a cohesive foundation for learning, teaching, and assessment at Joe Hall. Thinking Maps provide another foundation for change and continuity through the grade levels for students, but they also provide a common language throughout the whole school for thinking and sharing content knowledge.

A brief tour of the school shows that this synthesis of approaches is quite visible. In the library, a banner across the back of the room proclaims the core knowledge slogan: "What every student needs to know in order to succeed." Taped on the end of every standing bookshelf are examples of students' work. Each bookshelf had become a billboard for a certain grade level.

The content knowledge—*what* every student should know—is organized and synthesized, using Thinking Maps for *how* every student could come to know content at every grade level. Attached to the pages are students' products, such as writing, from the mapping of "core" knowledge. Moving out of the library, I found thinking visible everywhere, in all classrooms.

A kindergarten/1st grade combination classroom works with the teacher to create a Flow Map of the events of the Boston Tea Party on the chalkboard. Students then copy the maps onto a long piece of construction paper and fold it so it stands on their desks. Each student is writing her own description of the historical event.

In a 2nd grade classroom down the hallway, one teacher at the board facilitates a discussion about the similarities and differences between Presidents Lincoln and Washington. A Double Bubble Map is slowly being constructed on the chalkboard to capture students' ideas. Another teacher is moving from table to table, facilitating students' efforts as they create their own maps. These are team teachers, who have combined classrooms. They work so closely together that they describe themselves "as good as married." The students are actively engaged because they have used this map before. This is evidenced as the roaming teacher, obviously full of pride, pulls out a student's Writing-Thinking Maps portfolio from a file box on a side counter. A quick review shows the development of this student's capacity to organize his thinking for structuring the final drafts that are stapled to the maps.

In a 3rd grade class across the center courtyard of the school, the students have worked in cooperative groups to create large "explorer cubes." The groups research a famous world explorer. They paste some form of information on each of the six sides of the cube: pictures, written summaries, geographic maps, and various Thinking Maps for organizing details about the explorers. Right next to this class is a Mathematics Lab. Three students are sitting at a table with a specialist, working through a simple word problem about adding apples and oranges. The specialist realizes that the students are having a difficult time abstracting the most relevant information from a paragraph. She first guides students using the Tree Map to sort the types of information in the problem into categories. Then she uses a Circle Map to focus on defining the problem.

In a portable classroom in a far corner of the school, 4th graders are using a technique for reading comprehension called "the reading ladder." These are colorful booklets of five or six pages, each of varying length, stapled together so that the shortest is on top, the longest at the bottom. It is an effective replacement of a book report that makes it easy to flip the pages to see another depiction of information about the story. Students embellish each page with writing, drawings, and, most recently, Thinking Maps. The first page might be for sequencing the plot, using a Flow Map. This is followed by character descriptions, comparisons, main idea, and causes and effects of actions, each respectively displayed with a Thinking Map.

In a 5th grade class close to the main office, students have developed fluency with all of the Thinking Maps and are discussing what sequence of Maps would be most useful for organizing ideas for writing a persuasive paper. They differ in their choices, but most students end up using the Multi-Flow Map for showing causes and effects, a Tree Map for organizing their main argument and supporting evidence, and a Flow Map to sequence their paragraphs.

Back in the principal's office, Barbara is already building the next strong link in a chain. She thinks about change as linking new approaches together over several years, not single school years, and how that affects the whole school. She wants to talk about this new idea; but first, she summarizes her view of how Thinking Maps have provided one more link in the chain:

> The key to the success of this approach is the common thinking-process vocabulary and the visual language provided by the Thinking Maps. It is particularly difficult to find strategies that work together to develop higher-order thinking skills. I believe that the teachers embraced these maps because they are easily learned, and the teachers have incorporated each map directly into their everyday classroom activities. Additionally, Thinking Maps are used across grade levels, from kindergarten on up; and our bilingual and English-as-a-second-language students were successful with these strategies because they were also reinforced across the whole school.

Then Barbara turns to her newest investment of time, energy, and human resources: the installation of IBM computers in almost every classroom and the staff training that will occur over the following years. Accompanying software includes a writing program, and she wants to know how the Thinking Maps and school-wide writing portfolios will link with the IBM approach. She is already thinking through how this technology will become part of the teacher change process in a complex, growing, learning organization that builds continuity as it matures.

Integrating Teaching, Learning, and Assessment Tools for Constructive Teaching and Learning

These two portraits, and that of Norm Schuman's classroom in the first chapter, highlight the essential elements of how visual forms can become integrated into very different classrooms and schools as constructivist tools for teaching and learning. But why now in the 1990s? These applications by students, teachers, and principals may only have been possible through a basic shift in understandings of the constructive nature of the learning process. As one of the students in Frank Draper's class understood, educators are beginning to discard the "old school" worksheets and instead build new learning environments that are rigorous and interesting for students. This is because students are having to take the responsibility for actively constructing their own mental models of knowledge, using student-centered tools for learning.

Constructivism is based on students' seeking out and making connections and interconnections *on their own*. Lori Shepard summarizes this view, if not this whole book:

The notion that learning comes about by the accretion of little bits is outmoded learning theory. Current models of learning based on cognitive psychology contend that learners gain understanding when they construct their own knowledge and develop their own cognitive maps of the interconnections among facts and concepts (1988/1989, pp. 5–6).

This often unwieldy, undefinable concept of *interconnectiveness* is the underlying foundation for schools' shifts toward constructivism, new (visual) technologies, and interactivity in relationships in schools. Now we are developing rigorous visual tools that help bring definition to the phrase "making connections within and across disciplines."

In the three portraits, students construct knowledge by connecting facts and concepts; they create final products by using visual tools to transform information. Participants in these learning environments are communicating using these same tools with the support of visual technologies. For example, groups of students are giving oral presentations using an overhead projector in Norm Schuman's class; Barbara Bell is communicating with the whole school via closed circuit television; and students in Frank's class are huddled around computers, making feedback loops and manipulating variables in a faraway ecosystem.

Visual tools provide a common interactive framework for inclusive classrooms, for multiage settings, and for cooperative learning and small-group projects, as well as a common language for schoolwide learning. Importantly, these visual tools are integrated into other teaching and learning processes as everyday practical tools, not as a forced procedure or model that does not fit the needs of the classroom participants.

Visual Tools for Continuous Assessment

The type of critical self-examination educators have taken on in the past decade has raised questions about the values of outcomes we have previously established for students, indicating the need for change in teaching, learning, and assessment. In particular, increased attention is being focused on "process" assessment, requiring that it move closer to student learning by employing multiple measures, including samples of student work that are collected in context and based on authentic tasks. These types of assessment steer teaching and learning toward the outcome of developing self-reliant, self-confident, self-reflective adults who can make decisions in a social context.

As these views of assessment measures evolve, educators seek tools to complement and expand the types and forms of information learned about students from standardized tests. Whereas standardized tests provide a quantitative "snapshot" of student achievement, assessment tools such as portfolios, performance tasks, and student exhibits offer a more qualitative "videotape." Yet, even with the measurement of performance tasks or portfolios, educators are staying within the confines of assessment being an end-product form rather

than a continuous progression, a spiral-like, in-the-moment process.

This is where visual tools are especially helpful, not necessarily as end products, but as ever-changing, accessible maps for how and what a student is thinking. They make what is implicit, explicit, by providing a graphic artifact of a student's cognition. So often educators describe thinking as completely invisible, something that happens in the "black box" of the mind. But as John Clarke notes, student-made maps have "the advantage of remaining visible, even after the learning and thinking have occurred" (Clarke 1991, p. 292).

And what is visible? Whether it's a brainstorming web, task-specific organizer, or thinking-process map, both students and teachers have a *visual crossroads* for the content being expressed *and* the processes by which connections are being constructed. This visibility leads both student and teacher to assess the connectiveness of knowledge in the moment. Teachers can then use the maps to monitor and mediate students' developing complexity of conceptual understandings and their levels of sophistication with certain key thinking processes. Further, visual tools document one's ability to organize patterns of information, choose from a range of patterns, and illustrate relationships based on these understandings. They enable both teachers and students to reflect on and discuss ways of processing information.

As the two portraits in this chapter reveal, when visual tools are used over time, teachers ultimately are faced with a new form in which to see knowledge—their own and their students' views. As students use visual tools, teachers can see the developing ideas and concepts—and how an individual student is putting things together—and thus have a new means for assessing learning in the progress of instruction. Shepard (1988/1989) captures this view of developing knowledge:

> Beginners' knowledge is spotty and superficial, but as learning progresses, understanding becomes integrated and structured. Thus, assessment should tap the connectedness of concepts and the student's ability to access "interrelated chunks."

By using visual tools, a teacher simultaneously has *access to* and may *assess* both the "content" knowledge and the "processes" that a student is employing to come to a new understanding. Is the student's content knowledge weak, or is the thinking and reasoning problematic? Or both? This unification of content and process—shown by the interconnectiveness of ideas—reveals a unique dimension of these tools. Visual tools thus provide beginning and midrange windows into the thinking, concepts, and misconceptions of the student so that the teacher—and students themselves—may remedy a problem and encourage new connections on the pathway to the final product.

Tools for Organizational Learning

> We are coming to understand the importance of relationships and non-linear connections as the source of new knowledge. Our task is to create organizational forms that facilitate these processes (Wheatley 1992).

The phrase "learning organizations" has captured the imagination of business leaders and educators within the past few years. This term is often confused by those of us in education because we describe our schools, quite naturally, as organizations for learning, or learning communities. But the basic meaning of a learning organization, as described by Peter Senge, is "an organization that is continually expanding its capacity to create its future" (1990, p. 14). Of course, by definition, every school is an organization for student learning, but not necessarily structured as an organization that is learning about and changing itself for future benefits.

It is no coincidence that two of the newest vehicles for school change come directly from the business world: Total Quality Management and systems thinking. Both of these approaches draw heavily from the use of visual tools but are not necessarily dependent on them. TQM uses a mix of traditional graphs and matrixes and dynamic visual tools much like those presented in this book, called "transformation tools" (Bonstingl 1992). In the systems dynamics field, feedback loop diagramming and related graphs also play an important part in the process of seeking to understand the interconnections and interdependencies within a system.

The central theme in this book is the interconnection between a new *theory* of learning called constructivism, new *methods* (embedded in new technologies and interactive learning), and new visual *tools* for constructing knowledge. In the *Fifth Discipline Fieldbook*, Peter Senge and his coauthors summarize the interrelationships among theory, methods, and tools as related to the business world:

> New theories penetrate into the world of practical affairs when they are translated into methods and tools...."Tool" comes from a prehistoric Germanic word for "to make, to prepare, or to do." It still carries that meaning: tools are what you make, prepare, or do with (Senge et al. 1994).

It is today's students who will construct new knowledge. As we come more and more to believe that knowledge is not only interconnected but also interdependent, then we will see how much we need to provide students with dynamic new mental tools. These tools will help them unlearn and relearn what we have taught them so that they may build new theories of knowledge and also have the experience and capacity to create new tools for making their world.

References

Works Cited in Text

Armbruster, B.B., T.H. Anderson, and J. Ostertag. (1987). "Does Text Structure/Summarization Instruction Facilitate Learning from Expository Text?" *Reading Research Quarterly* 22, 3: 331–346.

Armbruster, B.B., T.H. Anderson, and J. Ostertag. (November 1989). "Teaching Text Structure to Improve Reading and Writing." *The Reading Teacher* 43, 2: 130–137.

Ausubel, D. (1978). "In Defense of Advance Organizers: A Reply to the Critics." *Review of Educational Research* 48, 2: 251–257.

Baratta-Lorton, R. (1977). *Mathematics…A Way of Thinking.* Menlo Park, Calif.: Addison-Wesley.

Bloom, B.S., ed. (1956). *Taxonomy of Educational Objectives. Handbook I: Cognitive Domain.* New York: McKay.

Bonstingl, J.J. (1992). *Schools of Quality.* Alexandria, Va.: Association for Supervision and Curriculum Development.

Brooks, J.G., and M.G. Brooks. (1993). *The Case for Constructivist Classrooms.* Alexandria, Va.: Association for Supervision and Curriculum Development.

Buzan, T. (1979). *Use Both Sides of Your Brain.* New York: E.P. Dutton.

Caine, R.N., and G. Caine. (1991). *Making Connections: Teaching and the Human Brain.* Alexandria, Va.: Association for Supervision and Curriculum Development.

Citron, H., and J. Glade. (1985). "Strategic Reasoning." In *Developing Minds,* edited by A.L. Costa. Alexandria, Va.: Association for Supervision and Curriculum Development.

Clarke, J.H. (1991). *Patterns of Thinking.* Needham Heights, Mass.: Allyn and Bacon.

Costa, A.L., ed. (1985). *Developing Minds.* 1st ed. Alexandria, Va.: Association for Supervision and Curriculum Development.

Costa, A.L., ed. (1991). *Developing Minds.* 2nd ed. Alexandria, Va.: Association for Supervision and Curriculum Development.

Cronin, H., D. Meadows, and R. Sinatra. (September 1990). "Integrating Computers, Reading, and Writing Across the Curriculum." *Educational Leadership* 48, 1: 57–62.

CTB/McGraw-Hill. (1996). *English Language Arts Assessment.* New York: Author.

deBono, E. (1970). *Lateral Thinking.* New York: Harper and Row.

Fauconnier, G. (1985). *Mental Spaces.* Cambridge, Mass.: MIT Press.

Fillmore, C. (1986). "Frames and the Semantics of Understanding." *Quaderni di Semantica* 6, 2: 222–253.

Fogarty, R., and J. Bellanca. (1991). *Patterns for Thinking.* Palatine, Ill.: I.R.I. Group.

Gage, N.L. (1974). *Teacher Effectiveness and Teacher Education: The Search for a Scientific Basis.* Palo Alto, Calif.: Pacific Books.

Gardner, H. (1983). *Frames of Mind.* New York: Basic Books, Inc.

Gardner, H. (1985). *The Mind's New Science.* New York: Basic Books, Inc.

Hechinger, F.M. (June 27, 1960). "Student I.Q.'s Rise in California Tests." *The New York Times*, p. 1.

Hyerle, D. (1988–1993). *Expand Your Thinking* (Series: Pre-K–Grade 8). Cary, N.C.: Innovative Sciences, Inc.

Hyerle, D. (1990). *Designs for Thinking Connectively.* Lyme, N.H.: Designs for Thinking.

Hyerle, D. (1991). "Expand Your Thinking." In *Developing Minds*, 2nd ed., edited by A.L. Costa. Alexandria, Va.: Association for Supervision and Curriculum Development.

Hyerle, D.N. (1993). "Thinking Maps as Tools for Multiple Modes of Understanding." Unpublished doctoral diss., University of California, Berkeley.

Hyerle, D. (1995). *Thinking Maps: Tools for Learning.* Cary, N.C.: Innovative Sciences, Inc.

Hyerle, D. (December 1995/January 1996). "Thinking Maps: Seeing Is Understanding." *Educational Leadership* 53, 4: 85–89.

International Reading Association. (1988). *New Directions in Reading Instruction.* Newark, Del.: Author.

Jacobs, H.H., ed. (1989). *Interdisciplinary Curriculum: Design and Implementation.* Alexandria, Va.: Association for Supervision and Curriculum Development.

Johnson-Laird, P.N. (1983). *Mental Models.* Cambridge, Mass.: Harvard University Press.

Jones, B.F., J. Pierce, and B. Hunter. (December 1988/January 1989). "Teaching Students to Construct Graphic Representations." *Educational Leadership* 46, 4: 20–25.

Lakoff, G. (1987). *Women, Fire, and Dangerous Things.* Chicago: University of Chicago Press.

Lipman, M. (1985). "Philosophy for Children." In *Developing Minds*, edited by A.L. Costa. Alexandria, Va.: Association for Supervision and Curriculum Development.

Lipman, M. (1991). *Thinking in Education.* Cambridge, England: Cambridge University Press.

Margolies, N. (1991). *Mapping Inner Space.* Tucson, Ariz.: Zephyr Press.

Marzano, R.J. (1992). *A Different Kind of Classroom: Teaching with Dimensions of Learning.* Alexandria, Va.: Association for Supervision and Curriculum Development.

McKenzie, J. (January/February 1996). "Grazing the Net." *From Now On: The Educational Technology Journal* 5, 5: n.p. (http://www.pacificrim.net/~mckenzie/grazing1.html; e-mail, mckenzie@pacificrim.net).

McTighe, J., and F.T. Lyman Jr. (April 1988). "Cueing Thinking in the Classroom: The Promise of Theory-Embedded Tools." *Educational Leadership* 45, 7: 18–24.

National Council of Teachers of Mathematics. (1990). *Curriculum and Evaluation Standards.* Washington, D.C.: Author.

Novak, J.D., and B.D. Gowin. (1984). *Learning How to Learn.* Cambridge, England: Cambridge University Press.

Parks, S., and H. Black. (1992). *Organizing Thinking, Book I.* Pacific Grove, Calif.: Critical Thinking Press & Software.

Perkins, D.N., and G. Soloman. (1989). "Are Cognitive Skills Context-Bound?" *Educational Researcher* 8, 1: 16–25.

Richmond, B., S. Peterson, and P. Vescuso. (1987/1991). *STELLA.* Lyme, N.H.: High Performance Systems.

Rico, G.L. (1983). *Writing the Natural Way.* Los Angeles: J.P. Tarcher, Inc.

Robinson, A.H. (1982). *Early Thematic Mapping in the History of Cartography.* Chicago: University of Chicago Press.

Rowe, M. (1974). "Wait Time and Rewards as Instructional Variables: Their Influence on Language, Logic and Fate Control." *Journal of Research in Science Teaching* 11: 81–94.

Samson, R. (1975). *Thinking Skills.* Stamford, Conn.: Innovative Sciences, Inc.

Senge, P.M. (1990). *The Fifth Discipline.* New York: Currency Doubleday.

Senge, P., C. Roberts, R.B. Ross, B.J. Smith, and A. Kleiner. (1994). *The Fifth Discipline Fieldbook.* New York: Currency Doubleday.

Shepard, L. (April 1989). "Why We Need Better Assessments." *Educational Leadership* 46, 7: 4–9.

Sinatra, R. (1994). *Improving Narrative Understanding and Writing for At-Risk Fourth Graders.* St. John's University. Jamaica, N.Y.

Snyder, T. (March 1994). "Blinded by Science." *The Executive Educator* 16, 3: 36–40.

Sylwester, R. (1995). *A Celebration of Neurons: An Educator's Guide to the Human Brain.* Alexandria, Va.: Association for Supervision and Curriculum Development.

Tufte, E.R. (1990). *Envisioning Information.* Cheshire, Conn.: Graphics Press.

Upton, A. (1941/1960). *Design for Thinking.* Palo Alto, Calif.: Pacific Books.

Upton, A., R. Samson, and A.D. Farmer. (1961). *Creative Analysis.* New York: E.P. Dutton.

Wandersee, J.H. (1990). "Concept Mapping and the Cartography of Cognition." *Journal of Research in Science Teaching* 27, 10: 923–936.

Wheatley, M.J. (1992). *Leadership and the New Science.* San Francisco: Berrett-Koehler Publishers, Inc.

Whimbey, A. (1995). *Analytical Reading and Reasoning.* 2nd ed. Cary, N.C.: Innovative Sciences, Inc.

Worsham, A., and G. Austin. (November 1983). "Effects of Teaching Thinking Skills on SAT Scores." *Educational Leadership* 41, 3: 50–51.

Wycoff, J. (1991). *Mindmapping.* New York: Berkley Book.

Bibliography

Ausubel, D. (1968). *Educational Psychology: A Cognitive View.* New York: Holt, Rinehart, and Winston.

Belenky, M.F., B.M. Clinchy, N.R. Goldberger, and J.M. Tarule. (1986). *Women's Ways of Knowing.* New York: Basic Books, Inc.

Bellanca, J. (1990). *The Cooperative Think Tank.* Palatine, Ill.: Skylight Publishing.

Berman, S. (1991). "Thinking in Context: Teaching for Openmindedness and Critical Understanding." In *Developing Minds,* edited by A.L. Costa. Alexandria, Va.: Association for Supervision and Curriculum Development.

Costa, A.L., and L.F. Lowery. (1989). *Techniques for Teaching Thinking.* Pacific Grove, Calif.: Midwest Publications.

Edwards, B. (1979). *Drawing on the Right Side of the Brain.* Los Angeles: J.P. Tarcher, Inc.

Gilligan, C. (1982). *In a Different Voice.* Cambridge, Mass.: Harvard University Press.

Goodlad, J.I. (1984). *A Place Called School.* New York: McGraw-Hill.

Gould, S.J. (1981). *The Mismeasure of Man.* New York: W.W. Norton and Company.

Guilford, J.P. (1967). *The Nature of Human Intelligence.* New York: McGraw-Hill.

Hart, L. (1983). *Human Brain and Human Learning.* New Rochelle: Brain Age Publishers.

Heath, S.B. (1983). *Ways with Words.* Cambridge, England: Cambridge University Press.

Helfgott, D., M. Helfgott, and B. Hoof. (1992). *Inspiration Software, User's Manual.* Portland, Ore.: Inspiration Software, Inc.

Inhelder, B., and J. Piaget. (1964). *The Early Growth of Logic in the Child.* New York: Norton.

Institute for Staff Development. (1971). *Hilda Taba Teaching Strategies Program (Unit 1, Elementary Ed.).* Miami, Fla.: Author.

Johnson, D.W., R.T. Johnson, E.J. Holubec, and P. Roy. (1988). *Circles of Learning: Cooperation in the Classroom.* Alexandria, Va.: Association for Supervision and Curriculum Development.

Kreidler, W.J. (1984). *Creative Conflict Resolution.* Glenview, Ill.: Scott, Foresman, and Company.

Kuhn, T.S. (1962). *The Structure of Scientific Revolutions.* Chicago: University of Chicago Press.

Lakoff, G., and M. Johnson. (1980). *Metaphors We Live By.* Chicago: University of Chicago Press.

Luria, A.R. (1976). *Cognitive Development.* Cambridge, Mass.: Harvard University Press.

Maclean, P. (1978). "A Mind of Three Minds: Educating the Triune Brain." In *Education and the*

Brain, edited by J. Chall. Chicago: University of Chicago Press.

Marr, E.G., J.A. Kovacs, and W.R. Sager. (1986). *Cognitive Skills Manual.* Seattle, Wash.: Training House, Inc.

Mensh, E., and H. Mensh. (1991). *The IQ Mythology.* Carbondale, Ill.: Southern Illinois University Press.

North Carolina State Department of Education. "North Carolina Standard Course of Study." (1991). Raleigh, N.C.: Author.

Palincsar, A.S., and A.L. Brown. (1984). "Reciprocal Teaching of Comprehension-Fostering and Comprehension-Monitoring Activities." *Cognition and Instruction* 1: 117–175.

Resnick, L.B., and L.E. Klopfer. (1989). *Toward the Thinking Curriculum: Current Cognitive Research.* Alexandria, Va.: Association for Supervision and Curriculum Development.

Rorty, R. (1979). *Philosophy and the Mirror of Nature.* Princeton, N.J.: Princeton University Press.

Rumelhardt, D.E. (1984). "Schemata and the Cognitive System." In *Handbook of Social Cognition,* edited by R.S. Wier and T.K. Krull. Hillsdale, N.J.: Lawrence Erlbaum, Associates.

Saphier, J., and R. Gower. (1987). *The Skillful Teacher.* Carlisle, Mass.: Research for Better Teaching.

Shoenfeld, A.H. (1985). *Mathematical Problem Solving.* New York: Academic Press.

Sternberg, R. (1990). *Metaphors of Mind.* Cambridge, England: Press Syndicate of the University of Cambridge.

Thinking Maps Software. (in press). Cary, N.C.: Innovative Sciences, Inc.

Vacca, R.T., and J.L. Vacca. (1989). *Content Area Reading.* 3rd ed. Glenview, Ill.: Scott Foresman.

von Glaserfeld, E. (1989). *Cognition, Construction of Knowledge, and Teaching.* The Netherlands: Kluwer Academic Publishers.

Vygotsky, L.S. (1936/1986). *Thought and Language.* Cambridge, Mass.: MIT Press.

Selected Resources for Visual Tools

Here is a short list of resources that include teacher texts, student materials, software, and professional development opportunities for bringing different types of visual tools into schools.

Chapter 3: Brainstorming Webs

Inspiration Software[TM]. High-quality brainstorming web capabilities and other organizing tools for upper elementary students through adult learning. Address: Inspiration Software, Inc., P.O. Box 1629, Portland, OR 97207. Phone: (503) 245-9011.

Mapping Inner Space, by Nancy Marguiles. Zephyr Press, publishers. A text for K–12 educators for applying mindmapping in classrooms. Professional development opportunities available. Address: Zephyr Press, P.O. Box 66006, Tucson, AZ 85728-6006. Phone: (520) 322-5090.

Use Both Sides of Your Brain, by Tony Buzan. E.P. Dutton, publisher. A basic text for mindmapping techniques for all ages. Address: Buzan Centre, Cardigan House, Suite 2, 37 Waterloo Rd., Winton Bournemouth, Dorset, UK BH91BD.

Chapter 4: Task-Specific Organizers

MacMapper software and materials by Richard Sinatra. Reading and writing materials with accompanying software for applying task-specific and thinking-process maps to learning. Professional development opportunities available. Address: St. Johns University, Grand Central & Utopia Pkwys., Jamaica, NY 11439. Phone: (718) 990-6205.

Patterns of Thinking, by John Clarke. Allyn and Bacon, publisher. A comprehensive theoretical and practical text for educators who want a foundation in "graphic organizers" and thinking process maps. Address: Department of Education, 533 Waterman Bldg., University of Vermont, Burlington, VT 05405. Phone: (802) 656-3356.

Chapter 5: Thinking-Process Maps

Learning How to Learn, by Joseph Novak and Bob Gowin. Cambridge University Press, publisher. A theoretical text with practical guidelines for implementing and assessing concept maps. Address: Department of Education, Cornell University, Kennedy Hall, Ithaca, NY 14853.

Organizing Thinking, Books I and II, by Sandra Parks and Howard Black. Critical Thinking Press and Software, publisher. A range of thinking skills-based maps, content application samples, and blackline masters. Professional development opportunities available. Address: Critical Thinking Press and Software, P.O. Box 448, Pacific Grove, CA 93950. Phone: 1-800-458-4849.

STELLA® software. High Performance Systems, publisher. Systems thinking software for advanced applications in business and education. Address: High Performance Systems, 45 Lyme Road, Hanover, NH 03755. Phone: (603) 643-9636.

Chapter 6: Thinking Maps®

Thinking Maps: Tools for Learning, by David Hyerle. Innovative Sciences, Inc., publisher. A comprehensive training guide for K–12 teachers for using Thinking Maps as a common visual language in whole schools. The Innovative Learning Group, a division of Innovative Sciences, also provides workshops and training-of-trainers seminars. Address: Innovative Learning Group, 975 Walnut Street, Suite 342, Cary, NC 27511. Phone: 1-800-243-9169. e-mail: ILG@valley.net

Thinking Maps: Software for the Mind (in press, available October 1996). A tool-based program with content area exercises for learning how to transfer Thinking Maps across disciplines. Address: See previous listing.

Index

A

add-on programs and materials, concerns about, 73
African American studies, 85
African ecosystems, 119–120, 124
algebra, 62
analogy, 105
Apple Computers, 120
artificial intelligence, 12, 16, 72
assessment, 29, 30, 49–50, 54, 67–70, 89–93, 112–116, 125–126
    alternative, 14, 91, 114, 121
    continuous, 125–126
    holistic scoring, 113–116
    holistic writing tests, 68
    informal, 49–50, 89, 114
    performance-based, 15, 125
    pre- and post-measures, 67, 68, 112
    process, 125
    standardized tests, 67, 68
    student interviews, 112–113
    teacher-made tests, 7–9
    use of rubrics, 68, 69, 92–93, 113
    validity considerations, 68, 113
    see also portfolios, self-assessment
auditory perceptions, 10
Ausubel, David, 80, 92, 93
auto repair, 78
automaticity, 64, 73, 78, 109

B

backmapping, 56, 58
Baratta-Lorton, R., 58
behaviorism, 13, 14
Bell, Barbara, 121–124
Bell curve, 72
biology, 74
Black, Howard, 76–78
blackline masters (or fill-in forms), 23–24, 54, 76

Bloom, Benjamin, 13, 51, 72, 97, 99
Bonstingl, J., 126
Brace Map, 101, 109, 110, 111
Braille map, 109
brain research, 11, 24, 25, 36, 72
brainstorming webs, vii, viii, 1, 15, 26, 27, 28, 35–50, 84
    and assessment, 49–50, 125
    and clustering, 38
    and constructivism, 37
    in cooperative learning, 44–45
    in individual learning, 43–44
    in schoolwide learning, 45–47
    software, 47–49
    uses of, 37–43
    see also visual tools
Bridge Map, 100, 101, 102, 103
Bubble Map, 101, 103, 107
burnout syndrome as a feedback system, 82
business
    learning environments in, 20, 87, 126
    sources of visual tools, 13, 127
    and teamwork, 35
Buzan, Tony, 36, 38–40, 47, 49, 96

C

cartography. *see* map-making
causal relationships, 82
cause-effect, 80, 89
Cause-Effect Map, 99
character maps, 68–70
chunking information, vii, 43
Circle Map, 97, 99, 101
Civil Rights movement, 85
Clarke, John, 24, 78–80, 91, 100, 105, 125
classification, 66, 85
classification diagram, 74, 75, 80
cognitive maps, 25
cognitive processes, 72
cognitive science, 10, 12, 13–15, 72, 73, 86, 105, 113
collaborative learning, xii, 19, 71
collaborative teaching, 64, 109
color in map-making, 8, 40, 46, 108
compare-contrast maps, 76–78
comparison of brainstorming webs, task-specific organizers,
    and thinking-process maps, 23–26, 73–74, 84–85, 125
computers, 15, 16, 109, 112, 118–121, 123, 124
    as information-delivery system and organizing tool, 17
    see also software, technology
concept circles, 60

concept mapping, 13, 22, 80, 81, 87, 91–93, 96
conflict resolution, 15, 19
consistency in the use of visual tools, 28, 99–100, 107, 110,
    113
consistency in the use of visual tools, *see also* schoolwide
    learning, and districtwide use of visual tools
constructivist theory of learning, vii-ix, 4, 13–15, 24–26, 33,
    37, 51–53, 72–76, 78, 80, 86, 93, 113, 118, 124–125, 126
content area, 87, 110, 120
content knowledge, 24, 25, 73, 78, 84, 89, 96, 126
Cooper, Brian, 47
cooperative learning, 7–9, 15, 18, 19, 22, 27, 32–33, 44–45,
    78, 85–86, 102, 103, 123, 124
Costa, Arthur, vii, 14, 72, 103, 105, 108
"The Country Mouse", 78
creativity, 10, 45, 46, 52, 76, 88, 100
cross-disciplinary uses of visual tools, 22, 46, 54–56, 74, 76,
    78–79, 82, 97, 109, 112, 124–125
cultural changes, 13
cultural knowledge, 46
curriculum design, 78, 86, 106, 112, 120–121
curriculum standards, 33–34
cyberspace, 51, 110

D

deBono, Edward, 14
decision-making process, xiii
deductive thinking. *see* thinking-process maps, Thinking
    Maps
Desk Map, 108
developmental learning and teaching, 72, 102, 107, 113
Dewey, John, 19
dialogical thinking. *see* thinking-process maps, Thinking
    Maps
dialogue, 23, 30, 45, 85, 86, 91, 99, 112
districtwide use of visual tools, 28, 64, 112
diversity, 19
Double Bubble Map, 101, 103, 107, 109, 122
Draper, Frank, 118–121, 124

E

economics, 39
empowerment, 120
English, 64, 84
English Language Arts Assessment, 68, 70
enjoyable learning activities, 45, 54, 97, 108
evaluation, end-product, 49, 91, 112–116
expectations for students, 28
experience, learning from, xiii, 19

F

feedback loops and flow maps, 80–82, 87, 93, 119, 124, 126
Feuerstein, Rueven, 13, 73
5th grade, 56, 123
1st grade, 86
fishbone diagrams, 76
flexibility. *see* consistency in the use of visual tools
Flow Map, 5, 101, 102, 103, 121, 123
flowcharts, 24, 25, 58, 65, 76, 85, 86, 87, 93
formative evaluation, 112
4th grade, 30
Frame, metacognitive, 101, 105, 110
frame questions, 55, 57

G

Gardner, Howard, 91
geographic maps, 10, 11, 123
geography, 56
geology, 56, 84
gifted students, 13
Gowin, Robert, 78–81, 91, 92, 93, 114
grade levels. *see* 1st grade, 2nd grade, etc.
graphic organizers. *see* task-specific organizers
graphic primitives, 95–102
graphics, 27, 47, 52, 58
graphs, 24

H

"Hagar the Horrible" (comic strip), 71
heterogenous classrooms. *see* inclusive classrooms and schools
hierarchical structures, 8, 53, 74, 80, 82, 84, 92, 96
High Performance Systems, 87, 120, 133
high-road transfer of thinking processes
        and content concepts, 74
        defined, 73
        and interdisciplinary investigations, 84, 85
        through flexible visual tools, 78, 84
        through thinking-process maps, 82, 103
        to new learning situations, 113
higher-order questions and skills, 8, 17, 72, 99
Hispanic students, 121
history, 122
history (social studies), 55
holistic assessment scoring, 97, 113–116
holistic learning, 11, 33, 46, 50, 60, 80, 93
homework, 30
human brain, 11
human intelligence, 12, 16
human population growth as a system, 88, 90
hypertext, 18

I

IBM computers, 123
inclusive classrooms and schools, 13, 32, 61, 97, 102, 124
individual learning, 32, 43–44, 61–63, 82–85
inductive thinking. *see* thinking-process maps, Thinking Maps
inductive tower, 78–79, 84, 85, 91, 93
Information Age, 13, 15, 71, 72, 113
information processing, 19, 52–54, 125
information storing, x
Information Superhighway, 16
Innovative Learning Group, 89, 133
instruction. *see* interdisciplinary instruction, and teacher
integration, of teaching, learning, and assessment, 4, 5, 6,
        124–126
integration of information, 56
intelligence
        artificial, 12, 16, 72
        human, 12, 16
interactivity, 19, 29
        see also cooperative learning, systems thinking
interdependence, xii
interdisciplinary instruction, 12, 15, 22, 28, 33, 40–43, 52,
        60, 82, 85, 93, 102, 103, 104, 110
International Reading Association, 56
inventing, xii
I.Q. testing, 72, 76

J

Jacobs, Heidi Hayes, 40–43
Jones, Frances Faircloth, v

K

K–9 content program, 106
K/W/L format, 112
kindergarten, 30, 86, 102, 105
kinesthetic perceptions, 10

L

Lakoff, George, 93
language arts, 24, 50, 76
language of visual tools. *see* Thinking Maps
learning organizations, 20, 123, 126–127
learning styles, 12
learning theories, 24, 80, 126
lifelong learning, xii, xiii, 83, 105, 107, 113, 117–129
linear thinking, 11, 12, 18, 36, 54, 56, 93
Lipman, Matthew, 14, 73
low-performing students, 56, 62
low-road transfer of thinking processes
        and content skills, 74

low road transfer of thinking processes (*continued*)
  defined, 73
  exhibited through student portfolios, 113
  through flexible visual tools, 84, 110
  by patterning, 78, 84, 103
  through thinking-process maps, 82

M
manupulatives in math, 60
map-making
  with color, 8, 40, 46, 108
  different perspectives of, 80
  geographical maps, 10, 11, 123
  mental maps, 10
  as metaphor, 9–11
  mindmaps, 40
  as problem solving, 110
  see also visual tools
Margolies, Nancy, 36
mathematics, 22, 58, 88, 102, 123
memorization, 52
mental models, 10, 22, 86, 88, 93, 105, 114
meta-tool, 101, 105
metacognition, ix, 23, 50, 74, 78, 86, 105, 112, 113
metacognitive frame (a visual tool), 101, 105, 110
metaphorical thinking. *see* thinking-process maps, Thinking
  Maps
mindmapping, 36, 39, 49
modeling the use of visual tools, 30
modeling the use of visual tools, *see also* teacher
motivation, 22–23
multi-age classrooms and schools, 102, 124
Multi-Flow Map, 100, 101, 103, 109, 123
multiple intelligences, 13, 14, 46, 91
multiple-level maps, 85

N
National Council of Teachers of Mathematics, 58
negotiating meanings, 32, 64, 71
nonlinear concepts and systems, 12, 17, 18, 36, 41–42, 46,
  52, 54, 80–82, 88, 93
North Carolina State Reading Test, 68–69
note making, 43, 46
Novak, Joseph, 78–81, 91, 92, 93, 114

O
organizational learning, 126
organizing information, 16, 17, 51–54, 125
Ornstein, Robert, 36

Osborn, Alex, 35
outcomes, 64
outlining, 53–55

P
Parks, Sandra, 76–78
part-whole reasoning, 80
patterns, 50, 52, 65, 66, 72, 74, 78, 80, 85, 86, 87, 102, 105
patterns, *see also* brain research
Paul, Richard, 14, 73
performance-based assessment, 15
Perkins, David, 14, 73, 78, 103
Peterson, Steve, 82
petroglyphs, x
physical education, 109
Piaget, Jean, 13, 14, 105
planning wheel, 41–42
portfolios, 7, 19, 50, 67, 113, 114, 121, 122, 123, 125
portraits of teachers using visual tools, 7–9, 118–121,
  121–124
Postman, Neil, 13
predictions, 88
presentations, 33
principal
  elementary school, 121–124
  middle school, 120–121
problem solving and problem solution, xi, 19, 35, 44, 46, 56,
  62, 63, 64, 83, 84, 85, 102, 110
professional development, 14, 28, 106, 107, 117, 123

Q
qualitative results of using visual tools, 22–23, 91, 96, 113
quantitative results of using visual tools, 22, 113
quantum physics, influence of in culture, 13
questions, higher-order, 2, 8, 17, 72, 99

R
reading, 22, 30, 31, 54–56, 65–67, 68, 78–79, 84, 102, 103,
  109, 123
reciprocal learning, xi
"The Red Wheelbarrow", 78
reflective learning, 32, 86, 112
research, 85–86, 120
resources, 132–134
restructuring schools, 12
Richmond, Barry, 82, 87
Rico, Gabriele Lusser, 37–38, 47
"rubber map", 80
rubrics, 68, 92–93, 113

S

Samson, Richard, 105, 106
scaffolding learning, 41, 50, 56, 84
Scholastic Assessment Test (SAT), 76
school level
    elementary, 7–9, 64, 78–79, 87, 109, 121–124
    K–9, 106
    lower elementary, 29, 30, 58, 78–79, 86, 102
    middle school, 118–121
    secondary, 29, 47, 64, 85, 86, 87, 109
    upper elementary, 29, 47
school-to-work transition, 19
schoolwide learning, 28, 45–47, 64–65, 86–87, 97, 106
Schuman, Norm, 7–9, 33, 118, 124
science, 22, 50, 60, 78
scientific process, 64, 67, 76, 102, 120
2nd grade, 86, 122
self-assessment, 23, 32, 33, 50, 67, 105, 113
self-worth, 46
semantic maps, 23, 24, 36, 65, 66
semantics, 74, 105
Senge, Peter, 81–82, 126–127
sequencing, 80
Sequencing Map, 99
Shepard, Lori, 124, 126
Sinatra, Richard, 65, 66
6th grade, 7–9, 56
skills, process, 24, 73, 126
social sciences, 56
social studies, 7–9, 50, 56, 74, 102
software
    Inspiration, 45, 47–49
    MacMapper, 65–67, 87
    STELLA, 82, 87–90, 96, 118, 120
    teacher-created, 119
    Thinking Maps, 87, 109–112, 121–124
    see also resources
Soloman, Gabriele, 73, 78, 103
sorting tree, 58, 59
special education students, 13, 62
    see also inclusive classrooms and schools
Sperry, Roger, 36
standardized tests, 22, 67, 96
    see also assessment
student-centered learning, 2, 18, 19, 85, 91, 109
students. *see* school level, grade levels (1st grade, 2nd grade, etc.)
summative evaluation, 112
supervision and observations, 109
systems thinking, x, 80–82, 87, 89, 93, 96, 119, 120
    see also thinking-process maps, Thinking Maps

T

Taba, Hilda, 13
task-specific organizers 15, 26, 26–29, 31, 51–70, 84
    across disciplines, 54–56
    and assessment, 67–70, 125
    and constructivism, 51–53
    in cooperative learning, 63–64
    in individual learning, 61–63
    as outlining structures, 53–54
    in schoolwide learning, 64–65
    software, 65–67
    uses of, 54–60
    see also visual tools
teacher
    as coach, 31, 50, 84
    as collaborator, 64, 109, 122
    as computer literate, 67, 118
    as constructivist practitioner, 60, 124–125
    as curriculum designer, 112
    as expert, 107
    as facilitator, 30–33, 45, 67, 78, 108, 122
    as implementor, 106–107
    as learner, 106–107, 125–127
    as mediator, 62, 113, 125
    as modeler, 31, 58–59, 84, 106, 107
    as presenter of a view of knowledge, 93
    as programmer, 118
    as questioner, 55, 107
    as reinforcer, 106
    as self-reflective adult, 125
teachers' concerns about add-on programs, 73
team teaching, 122
technology, 13, 15–18, 47, 71, 126
television, 16, 17
    closed-circuit, 121, 124
10th grade, 85
textbooks, 54, 64
think aloud, 44, 113
THINK! language arts program, 76, 106
Think-Pair-Share, 31, 63
Thinking Maps, 3–6, 95–116, 121, 123
    and assessment, 112–116
    background, 106–107
    characteristics of, 99–105
    compared with other visual tools, 96–97
    in cooperative learning, 108
    definitions of, 97–99, 101
    forerunner of, 76
    illustrations of, 98, 101
    implementation, 106–107

Thinking Maps (*continued*)
    in individual learning, 107–108
    as a language, 95–99, 105–106, 124–125
    in schoolwide learning, 106, 108–109, 121–124
    software, 109–112
    used across disciplines, 96, 102–103, 122–123
    see also visual tools
thinking skills, 2, 22, 72, 73, 78, 86
thinking-process maps, 15, 26–28, 49, 71–94, 96, 99
    and assessment, 89–93, 125
    compared with other visual tools, 73–74, 96–99
    and constructivitism, 71–74
    in cooperative learning, 85–86
    in schoolwide learning, 86–87, 107, 120
    software, 87–89, 120
    uses of, 74–82
    see also visual tools
3rd grade, 78–79, 103, 109, 110, 122
time savings, 32
Toffler, Alvin, 117
Total Quality Management (TQM), 121–122, 126
transfer of thinking processes. *see* low-road transfer and
    high-road transfer
Tree Map, 4, 27, 75–76, 85, 100, 101, 103, 104, 109, 115, 123
Tufte, Edward, 17
2001, A Space Odyssey, 18

U
underachievers, 8
Upton, Albert, 74–76, 105, 106

V
"Vee" diagram, 78–79
Venn diagrams, 60, 76
Vescuso, Peter, 82
video cameras, 15
videocassette recorders, 15
visual perceptions, 10

visual tools
    advantages of, 29–32
    choosing, 28–29
    consistency in the use of, 28, 97
    and constructivism, vii–ix, 24–26, 33
    for continuous assessment, 125–126
    and cooperative learning, 32–33
    cross-disciplinary uses of, 22, 46, 54–56, 74, 76, 78–79,
        97, 109, 112
    definition of, 21, 23–28
    as exhibits of student work, 122–124, 125
    as facilitators of conceptual development, 79–81
    and learning organizations, 126–127
    for lifelong learning, 117–127
    questions concerning, 27–29
    student ownership of, 29–32, 72, 107, 108
    as theory-embedded, 24–26
    types of, 24–29
    used in standardized tests, 68–70
    see also brainstorming webs, task-specific organizers,
        thinking-process maps, Thinking Maps
Vygotsky, L.S., 13, 14

W
wait time, 44
Wandersee, James H., 10, 60
Western view of the form of knowledge, 80
Wheatley, Margaret, 11, 15, 16, 126
Williams, William Carlos, 78
women's studies, 85
word processing, 47
workplace learning, 19, 102
workplace skills, 71, 109
writing, 2, 50, 66, 66–67, 107, 110, 113, 114
    persuasive, 123
    prewriting, 38
    process 15, 22, 24, 36, 46, 56, 65, 102
    see also holistic assessment scoring
Wycoff, Joyce, 38–39